Differentiating by Readiness

Strategies and Lesson Plans for Tiered Instruction Grades K-8

Joni Turville, Linda Allen, and LeAnn Nickelsen

EYE ON EDUCATION
6 DEPOT WAY WEST, SUITE 106
LARCHMONT, NY 10538
(914) 833–0551
(914) 833–0761 fax
www.eyeoneducation.com

A sincere effort has been made to supply the identity of those who have created specific strategies. Any omissions have been unintentional.

Library of Congress Cataloging-in-Publication Data

Turville, Joni.

  Differentiating by readiness : strategies and lesson plans for tiered instruction grades K-8 / Joni Turville, Linda Allen, and LeAnn Nickelsen.

     p. cm.

  ISBN 978-1-59667-137-9

  1. Active learning. 2. Lesson planning—Study and teaching (Elementary) 3. Cognitive styles in children—United States. I. Allen, Linda. II. Nickelsen, LeAnn. III. Title.

  LB1027.23.T87 2010

  371.39′4—dc22

                                                                                        2009037938

10 9 8 7 6 5 4 3 2 1

Also Available from EYE ON EDUCATION

Differentiating by Student Interest: Strategies & Lesson Plans
Joni Turville

**Differentiating by Student Learning Preferences:
Strategies & Lesson Plans**
Joni Turville

How the Best Teachers Differentiate Instruction
Elizabeth Breaux and Monique Boutte Magee

**Differentiated Instruction:
A Guide for Elementary School Teachers**
Amy Benjamin

**Differentiated Instruction for K-8 Math and Science:
Activities and Lesson Plans**
Mary Hamm and Dennis Adams

**Differentiating Assessment in Middle and High
School Mathematics and Science**
Sheryn Spencer Waterman

**Differentiating Assessment in Middle and High
School Mathematics and Science**
Sheryn Spencer Waterman

**Handbook on Differentiated Instruction for
Middle and High Schools**
Sheryn Spencer Northey

**Differentiated Assessment for Middle and
High School Classrooms**
Deborah Blaz

**Differentiated Instruction:
A Guide for Middle and High School Teachers**
Amy Benjamin

**Differentiated Instruction Using Technology:
A Guide for Middle and High School Teachers**
Amy Benjamin

The Democratic Differentiated Classroom
Sheryn Spencer Waterman

Dedication

To Brock and Brittany

Your amazing potential as human beings inspires me to strive
to be a better teacher every day. I love you so much.

JT

To Keaton and Aubrey

Thank you for teaching me so many valuable lessons in life. You truly have provided double the delight, double the laughter, and double the hugs and kisses.

Love you bestest bestest!

Your mom, LeAnn

To Mason, my first grandchild, and to Alex and Brandon, my grandsons-in-
heart. You have started a new season of teaching in my life. I love you.

Nan (lga)

About the Authors

Joni Turville is an award winning teacher and brings energy and expertise to both her presentations and instructional practice, which also includes working as a technology consultant, administrator, and university instructor. She has written numerous articles and books, focusing on effective instructional strategies, differentiated instruction, and technology. Joni is also passionate about professional development and has developed many train-the-trainer programs, as well as done significant work in using technology for professional development. She lives in Edmonton, Alberta, Canada, and is a popular local, national, and international presenter.

Linda G. Allen is an educational specialist, speaker, and writer. She works with both general education and special education teachers from kindergarten through high school, and provides training for substitute teachers, paraprofessionals, and parents. Her long-time interest in brain-compatible research has provided opportunities to extend her knowledge of brain-compatible strategies, of building communities of learners, and of teaching students with special needs. Her topics include memory strategies for learning, novelty in the classroom, stress and threat, and processing learning. Linda lives near Louisville, Kentucky on a daylily farm. She has a husband, one daughter, three sons, two daughter-in-hearts, and a new grandson, along with two spoiled dogs, lots of deer, turkey, groundhogs, spiders, and snakes.

LeAnn M. Nickelsen is a nationally recognized presenter, consultant, and author with a passion for the learning experience and those who lead it. Prior to founding Maximize Learning, LeAnn was a classroom educator and was awarded Teacher of the Year for her excellence in the classroom. She has written multiple books and frequently presents on a wide range of topics, including brain research, differentiation, deeper learning, reading and vocabulary strategies, and nutrition affecting cognition. She is known for delivering a wealth of information in an active, fun format with very specific, practical classroom examples. Her passions in life are raising her school-age twins and helping all students to maximize their learning opportunities. LeAnn and her family live in the beautiful, rolling hills of Ridgefield, Connecticut.

Acknowledgements

♦ Thanks to the wonderful people at Eye On Education, particularly to Bob Sickles, who facilitated our collaborative efforts, and has seen this three-book series to a conclusion.

♦ Thank you to Hyde Park, NY teachers for their valuable input on the tiered lesson plan.

♦ Thanks to Eric Jensen for taking the time to give us a quote to support the benefits of challenging each child where he/she is at.

♦ Thanks to Laura Smith, Olathe School District in Kansas, and JoAnn Blachford from St. Albert Protestant Schools in St. Albert, Alberta, for contributing to the chapter book/picture book list.

♦ Thanks to Lois Gluck for her wise feedback.

♦ Thanks to Paul Janzen for allowing us to use his analogy of Goldilocks for tiered instruction. The inspiration came while he was taking a graduate course on DI and was reading this night time story to his four-year-old daughter, Erinn.

♦ Thank you to Spencer Bergstrand for his amazing talent in the graphic art design of the construction site on p. 10 (The Learning Zone).

Free Downloads

Beginning on page 89, you'll find 23 Blackline Masters. Book buyers have permission to print out these Adobe Acrobat© documents and duplicate them to distribute to your students.

You can access these downloads by visiting Eye On Education's website: www.eyeon-education.com. Click on FREE Downloads or search or browse our website to find this book and then scroll down for downloading instructions.

You'll need your bookbuyer access code: **DIFFRE-7137-9**

Contents

About the Authors vii

Acknowledgements ix

Free Downloads xi

Introduction xvii

    Why This Book Was Written xvii

    What This Book Will Do For You xviii

1 Building the Foundation: What is Tiering in Differentiated Instruction? 1

    Differentiating Instruction 3

        Differentiating Content (Adjusting Materials and Supports for Learning Concepts) 3

        Differentiating Process (Making Sense and Meaning of Content) 5

        Differentiating Products (Showing What Has Been Learned) 5

    Defining Tiering 6

        How Tiering Is Framed in This Book 6

    Straight Talk on Tiering: What It Is and What It Isn't 7

        How Tiering and Response to Intervention Differ 8

    A Metaphor for Tiering: "The Learning Zone" 9

    Research to Support Tiering 11

        Zone of Proximal Development (Vygotsky, Rieber, and Carton) 11

            Implications for Differentiation 11

        The Effects of Challenge on the Brain (Jensen, Jacobs, and Diamond) 12

            Implications for Differentiation 12

        Applying Tiered Objectives with Gifted Talented Children (Kettler and Curliss) 12

            Implications for Differentiation 12

        Middle School Tiering (Richards and Omdal) 13

            Implications for Differentiation 13

        Tiering Instruction Using a Common Outcome (Witherell and McMackin) 13

            Implications for Differentiation 13

    Tying Things Together 14

2 The Essential Building Blocks: Getting Ready to Tier 15

    Activities That Celebrate Strengths and Encourage Growth 17

        Ask Me Poster 17

        Uniqueness Bingo 18

        My Strengths Web 19

        Children's Literature Connections 20

    Grouping and Tiered Instruction 22

    Cooperative Learning 23

        Before Grouping Strategies 23

        During Group Work Strategies 25

        After Grouping Strategies 26

    Bringing Parents On Board 26

    Tying Things Together 27

3 The Blueprint for Tiering: Designing with the End in Mind **29**
When to Tier 31
How to Set Up Tiering 32
Study Your Standards 32
Brainstorm Assessments and Implement Preassessments.................33
Types of Preassessments 34
Brainstorm Ways to Support Students with the Chosen Objectives 41
Tying Things Together 41

4 Pour the Concrete! It's Time to Tier **43**
Construction Specifications: The Tiered Lesson Plan Template 45
From Unit to the Daily Lesson Plan 45
The Big Picture 45
Preassessment 47
Materials 48
Grabber and Hook 48
Instruction 51
Writing the Objectives 51
The Three Tiers 53
Review the Tasks 55
Closure 55
Conduct the Lesson and Assess 56
Tiered Lesson Plan Examples 56
Tying Things Together 74

5 Passing Final Inspection: Assessment of Tiered Products **75**
How to Assess Tiered Assignments 77
Summative Assessment 77
Formative Assessment 77
Self-Checking 78
Self-Reflections 78
More Self-Reflection Ideas 79
"Dear Teacher" Notes 79
Two-Minute Quick Writes 79
Reflecting on the "Construction" of My Learning 80
Personal Reflection on Processing 80
Checklists 80
Cubing 81
Rubrics and Scoring Guides 82
Interviews and Conferences as Assessment Tools 82
What About Grading? 82
Tying Things Together 84

6 Cutting the Tape: Time to Start Tiering! **85**
Parting Words 87

Appendix: Blackline Masters **89**
Blackline Master 1: Uniqueness Bingo 91

Blackline Master 2a: My Learning Strengths at School..92
Blackline Master 2b: My Learning Strengths at Home 93
Blackline Master 3: ABC Brainstorm 94
Blackline Master 4: Task Assignment Details..95
Blackline Master 5: Learning Station Work Schedule 96
Blackline Master 6: Group Work Expectation Poster 97
Blackline Master 7: Group Task Cards for Younger Students...............................98
Blackline Master 8: Group Task Cards for Older Students..................................100
Blackline Master 9: Learning Contract—Group Work 102
Blackline Master 10: "Please Help" Tent Cards 104
Blackline Master 11: Classroom Noise Level Awareness.....................................105
Blackline Master 12: Group Work Self-Reflection for Younger Students 106
Blackline Master 13: Group Work Self-Reflection for Older Students................107
Blackline Master 14: Balancing Ways of Differentiating 108
Blackline Master 15: Anticipation Guide 109
Blackline Master 16: Door Pass..110
Blackline Master 17: H-Diagram 111
Blackline Master 18: W, W, W, W, and H Web 112
Blackline Master 19: Tiered Lesson Plan Template...113
Blackline Master 20: Bloom's Taxonomy Verbs From Top Down (1 of 2)...........114
Blackline Master 21: Product Choices..116
Blackline Master 22: Dear Teacher Notes..117
Blackline Master 23: Personal Reflection 118

References 121

Introduction

We don't receive wisdom; we must discover it for ourselves after a journey that no one can take for us.

—Marcel Proust

Students in today's classrooms are incredibly diverse. When teachers have a deep understanding of the philosophy of differentiated instruction (DI) they find effective ways to meet and exceed this wide range of students' needs. Children enter school with varied background knowledge, cultures, learning obstacles, personalities, learning strengths, energy levels, motivations, and ways of processing content.

One way to meet this challenge is through intentionally designed lessons. When preassessment or formative assessment shows that a student is ready for a deeper level of understanding, when the assessment shows that the student needs additional support, or when the assessment indicates additional strategies are necessary in order for the student to understand the new learning, it may be time to differentiate according to student readiness. The goal of this kind of teaching, called *tiered instruction*, is for all students to be appropriately challenged so that success and academic growth occurs. Tiering is just one way to differentiate instruction for student success but it's one of our favorite ways! Enjoy the journey this book will take you through.

Why This Book Was Written

Once upon a time there was a lovely, young student named Goldilocks. She was an adventurous sort, so one day she went walking through the forest in search of a teacher.

As Goldilocks rounded a bend in the path, she came into a bright clearing in the forest. She was very excited to find a teacher presenting a lesson that at first captured her attention. Goldilocks tried to stay engaged and learn, but she became frustrated as it was just too difficult. She sighed, waved goodbye to the first teacher, and continued on her way.

Goldilocks walked a bit longer and ambled up a hill where she found herself in a wide, flower-filled pasture. There a second teacher sat, seemingly waiting just for her. This teacher began her lesson, but Goldilocks soon became bored because it was just too easy. She waved goodbye to the second teacher, and once again went on her way.

Trudging through the forest more slowly now and less joyfully, she came across a magnificent meadow that was not only amazingly colorful but fragrant as well. There stood yet another teacher. The teacher began the lesson, and Goldilocks was enthralled! This lesson wasn't too hard! It wasn't too easy! It was just right!

This story illustrates the focus of tiered instruction—creating "just right" learning tasks and assessments for students so they can build on what they already know and can do, and continuously add layers of new learning while gaining personal confidence and learning strategies. A wide variety of practical strategies will be detailed because the goal of this book is to make tiering easier for you! The processes described will save you time in planning powerful, tiered lessons so that all students can be successful.

What This Book Will Do For You

You will be able to

- explain what tiering is and isn't, give a clear definition of the term, and implement tiered lesson plans within your classroom.

- use powerful preassessments to decide if, when, and how to tier your lessons and how to group your students effectively.

- understand ways to effectively have students work in small groups so they can accomplish the task successfully and responsibly.

- use the tiered lesson plan template to guide the planning of your tiered lessons.

- see a wide range of lesson plans and adapt some of them for your learners.

- understand how to assess and evaluate tiered objectives.

1

Building the Foundation: What is Tiering in Differentiated Instruction?

When we do the best we can, we never know what miracle is wrought in our life or the life of another.

—Helen Keller

When beginning to build a structure, we must create a solid foundation. Without it, no matter how creative or beautiful the structure is, it will eventually fall apart. When learning to tier instruction, it is important to have a deep understanding of differentiating instruction and how differentiating in this way is just one part of the process.

Differentiating Instruction

There are many different definitions of differentiated instruction. There doesn't seem to be one, specific way to describe it, but there are several factors that are important when adjusting instruction (Figure 1.1, page 4). We like the word "doable" to describe how to differentiate.

Differentiating begins with knowing your students. There are three things you can find out about them: what interests them, how they learn best, and how ready they are to learn a particular concept. Once you know these things about your students, you can adjust the content of what they are to learn. This is not to say that we can change the standards, but we can choose the kinds of materials they will use to learn and adjust the kinds of supports they may require to access the content. Next, the process of how they learn can be adjusted. This can incorporate things such as learning styles, multiple intelligences and cooperative learning. Finally, we can adjust the way students will demonstrate their learning by considering what products they will create or how they will show their learning.

Differentiating Content (Adjusting Materials and Supports for Learning Concepts)

♦ Resource materials are available at varying readability levels

♦ Audio and video clips

♦ Peer and adult mentors

♦ Keyed concepts and boldface typed vocabulary

♦ Ideas presented through a variety of tools (e.g., websites, audio books)

♦ Varied manipulatives and tools (e.g., charts, graphic organizers)

♦ Charts and models used to convey an idea

♦ Concrete objects used to explain abstract ideas

♦ Multimedia presentations including PowerPoint presentations

♦ Interest centers for additional exploration

♦ "I Wonder" statements to foster curiosity about current topics to guide mini-lessons, resources, and connections

♦ Events and interests in students' lives as examples in content areas

♦ Multiple intelligences and learning styles in exploring materials, especially considering auditory, visual, and kinesthetic modes

Figure 1.1. Differentiating Instruction

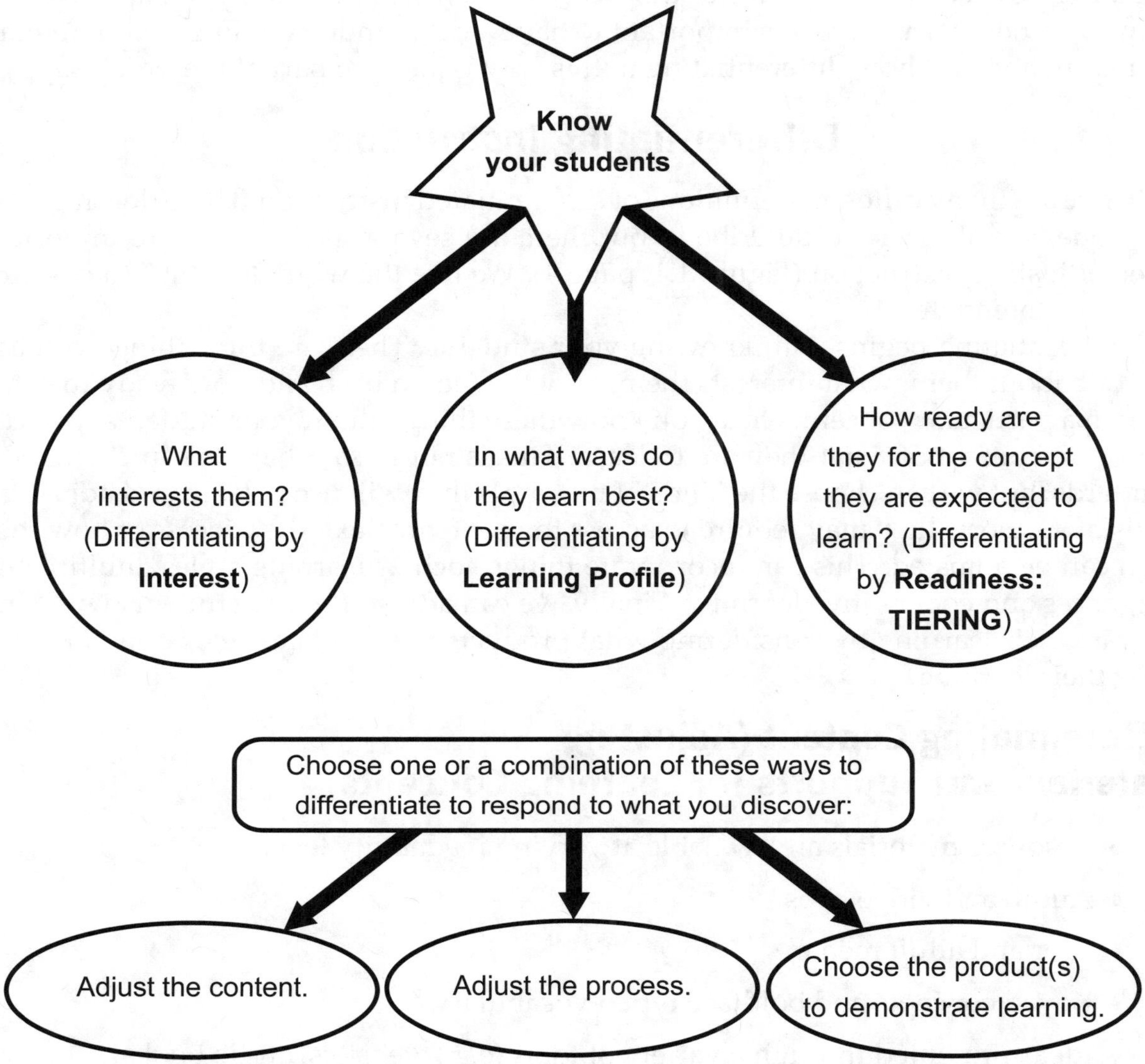

Know your students

What interests them? (Differentiating by **Interest**)

In what ways do they learn best? (Differentiating by **Learning Profile**)

How ready are they for the concept they are expected to learn? (Differentiating by **Readiness: TIERING**)

Choose one or a combination of these ways to differentiate to respond to what you discover:

Adjust the content.

Adjust the process.

Choose the product(s) to demonstrate learning.

Adapted from Tomlinson (2000)

- "Big picture" concept as well as the "step-by-step" understanding within each unit of study

- Text-to-speech software

Differentiating Process
(Making Sense and Meaning of Content)

- Leveled questions or question stems (different levels of complexity)

- Learning centers

- Personal agendas containing universal class assignments and supplementary or in-depth assignments for particular students

- Hands-on materials used in a variety of ways to build understanding of concepts

- Varied pace according to student's readiness and processing rate

- Literature circles, discussions, and Socratic seminars as ways to examine topics closely

- Cooperative learning tasks

- Choice in strategies for processing

- Varied working groups (partners, triads, small groups and alone)

- Use of WebQuests

- Choices for learning through activity structures such as RAFTs, choice boards, learning contracts, etc.

- Use of speech-to-text software

Differentiating Products
(Showing What Has Been Learned)

- Varied product choices that have options within the multiple intelligences and the learning styles, and considerations for gender, culture, and interests

- Technology-based products (e.g., digital photos, podcasts, blogs, wikis, multimedia presentations)

- Collaboration with art, music, physical education, and drama teachers to assist in the development of the criteria and quality assignments with students on various products for scoring guides and rubrics

- Use of student-designed rubrics to showcase criteria and levels of knowledge and understanding (with teacher input and guidance)

- Tiered product activities

Some of these ways to differentiate can be used as the basis for tiered assignments. Many can be used in combination, which further increases the complexity of planning, but may help to better meet student needs. For example, using resource materials at varying readability levels is a great way to help students understand important concepts. They could then be given leveled graphic organizers on which to process what they have read. In this way, both the content as well as the process are differentiated.

Defining Tiering

Tiering is used when there is a large gap between what students currently are able to do and what they are expected to learn. By providing extra support or challenge, students can all be successful in reaching the standard and have a high level of engagement. Tiering has been described in the literature in many ways and can be one of the most difficult parts of differentiated instruction to describe.

Adams and Pierce (2003) describe the tiered lesson structure as having multiple levels so students work in moderately challenging, but developmentally appropriate activities. "A tiered lesson addresses a particular standard, key concept and generalization but allows several pathways for students to arrive at an understanding of these components." They describe tiering as being qualitatively different, without simply adjusting quantity.

According to Heacox (2002), "Tiered assignments are differentiated learning tasks and projects that you develop based on your diagnosis of students' needs. When you use tiered assignments with flexible instructional groups, you are prescribing particular assignments to particular groups of students." She describes tiered lessons as a way to help match instruction to student needs.

Kingore (2005) relates the concept of tiering to having students work in greater depth in their understanding of a concept, as opposed to "treadmilling," where they are not progressing, but just doing more of the work they are already able to do.

Tomlinson (1999) writes that tiering is important when "students with different learning needs work with the same essential ideas and use the same key skills. The teacher designs activities so students all focus on the same concepts with different levels of complexity, abstractness and open-endedness." This increases the likelihood that all students learn and are challenged appropriately.

According to Wormeli (2007), tiering is related to a vertical, layered approach as opposed to a horizontal strategy. He combines this notion with Tomlinson's (1999) idea of the "equalizer," where these layers can be thought of in terms of things like complexity of thought, open-endedness and abstractness.

How Tiering Is Framed in This Book

In this book, tiering is defined as providing different learning activities when there is such a variance in readiness levels among the learners that students may not be able to learn effectively and be engaged if no adjustments are made. Tiered lessons are created based on the diagnosis of the students' needs. The goal is for all students to be appropriately challenged so that success occurs with each child. Learning is focused on the standards, and all students are expected to reach them, but with different kinds of support, complexity, and pacing.

Straight Talk on Tiering: What It Is and What It Isn't

In understanding tiered instruction, it is important to understand not only what it is, but what it is not. Figure 1.2 serves as a brief summary and it can help teachers focus on what they are planning and check whether it falls within the construct of tiering.

Figure 1.2. Is this Tiering?

Yes	No
◆ Begins with, and focuses on required standards	◆ May or may not be focused on standards
◆ Focuses on "big ideas" that will endure over time and be transferable to other subjects. All learners reach the same learning destination	◆ Standards are altered or not used. Care is not given to focus on enduring understanding
◆ Uses proactive instructional strategies, based on preassessments and ongoing formative assessments	◆ Reactive strategies after students have already experienced predictable frustration
◆ Fluid, constantly changing groupings, based on student needs	◆ Groups that stay the same for long periods of time or for the whole school year
◆ Tasks with increasing or decreasing complexity, abstractness or open-endedness; they are qualitatively different	◆ Adds or removes the volume (quantity) of work
◆ An indicator of a student's readiness to learn a particular concept	◆ An indicator of the ability or potential of the student
◆ Appropriate support or open-endedness provided for learners at all levels of readiness	◆ Support only for those who are "less ready"
◆ Creating as many tiers as necessary according to student preassessments	◆ Always three levels of tiering
◆ Equally engaging and challenging for all students	◆ Interesting, engaging tasks only for those who are most ready and tedious drill and practice for those who are less ready
◆ Encourages high levels of thinking for all students	◆ High-level thinking for only some tiers
◆ Strategically employed when there is a wide gap in readiness	◆ Used all day, every day

◆ Provides a wide range of support materials to suit different learners	◆ Uses limited kinds of support materials for learners
◆ Carefully structured tasks chosen by the teacher to suit learners	◆ Chaotic and disorganized
◆ All students involved in respectful and interesting tasks	◆ Only students who are most ready receive engaging tasks
◆ Groups vary in size according to student readiness	◆ Forced equal-size groups
◆ Assessing student strengths and using them to help students "learn how to learn"	◆ The creation of negative labels that will follow learners through all grades and subjects

How Tiering and Response to Intervention Differ

A different type of tiering is addressed within the *Individuals with Disabilities Education Act* (IDEA) of 2004. Embedded in IDEA is language that refers to intervention strategies for students who need an intentional, preventive plan for instruction and assessment in order to reach established benchmarks. This philosophy is called *Response to Intervention* (RTI) and is described in IDEA along with the students' responses to those intervention attempts. RTI is seen as a multilevel delivery of services, and these levels are also referred to as tiers. The tiers in RTI are structured differently than those within differentiated instruction and assessment.

The first level of RTI always includes the general core curriculum that all students receive. In this tier, 80 to 85% of the students will receive this information without additional assistance. The assessment that follows might indicate that the remainder of the students will need a secondary level (Tier 2) of targeted instruction to reach the established benchmarks. A third level (Tier 3) of instruction may be necessary if additional assessment reveals that the typical 3 to 6% of students are still in need of strategic interventions to support learning to reach the benchmark. RTI as it is currently defined applies mainly to reading comprehension and decoding, but some math and behavior is included. RTI also appears to intently address students with learning difficulties without including students whose needs tend to be on the gifted side.

In comparison, tiered instruction is based on the data gathered from a preassessment that indicates a student's readiness for new content and skills. The teacher then prepares to deliver instruction through various content materials and learning experiences so that all students move forward in their learning. Each student receives different instructional support and structure depending on their level, while still being challenged within his or her work. When the class is a heterogeneous mix of students with some students at a below-readiness level, then Tier 1 may include students who are involved in experiences that will increase their understanding so that they can more easily learn the new benchmark learning. Tier 2 then would be instruction for those students who come to the learning with the background knowledge and readiness skills ready to take on the objectives for the new benchmark learning. Tier 3 might include students who may be at the same readiness as another tier, but may need the learning delivered through more complex resources or through more complex processes. Tiered instruction involves all students, all content areas, and all readiness levels. Both RTI and tiered instruction are dependent on good assessment and accurate data collection (Council of Administrators of Special Education Inc., 2008).

A Metaphor for Tiering: "The Learning Zone"

The metaphor of a construction zone is one that fits tiered instruction well (Figure 1.3, page 10). Students must construct their own meaning with the help and guidance of the teacher who is the "architect" of learning. The teacher has the end goals and the standards in mind as the teacher plans to help the students reach those goals, and begins by placing that learning within the bigger picture. Through working on appropriately challenging tasks, the students will build enduring understandings (Wiggins & McTighe, 2005).

The description below details the metaphor of "The Learning Zone."

♦ Beginning at the bottom of the building, the foundation represents what the student brings to the learning (e.g., background knowledge: life experiences, culture, past curricular experience). We must anchor new learning to what students bring already stored in the brain.

♦ The teacher creates and refers to the blueprints in order to guide the learning. He or she has the skills and essential knowledge to create strong units and daily lessons in order to facilitate growth for where students are.

♦ The Learning Zone may consist of several levels of complexity. Students' learning is processed through these levels of complexity in order to master the standard and apply that learning to new situations.

♦ The escalator, elevator, and stairs represent the various routes students take to reach the standard.

♦ The scaffolding represents the support the teacher puts in place to help the students reach the standard. Sometimes the support is more or less depending on the needs of the students at that time.

♦ The "tools" to create the learning experience are the wide-ranging instructional experiences that the teacher uses to help students construct their understanding including "the building specifications" or the lesson plan template to guide the way for designing tiering, or even the "Diversity of Building Plans" where teachers can find a host of examples given.

♦ The teacher also functions as the building inspector by assessing progress and determining when students have reached the standards. This is done through preassessment and formative assessment that includes self-reflection, and summative assessments along the way.

Figure 1.3. The Learning Zone

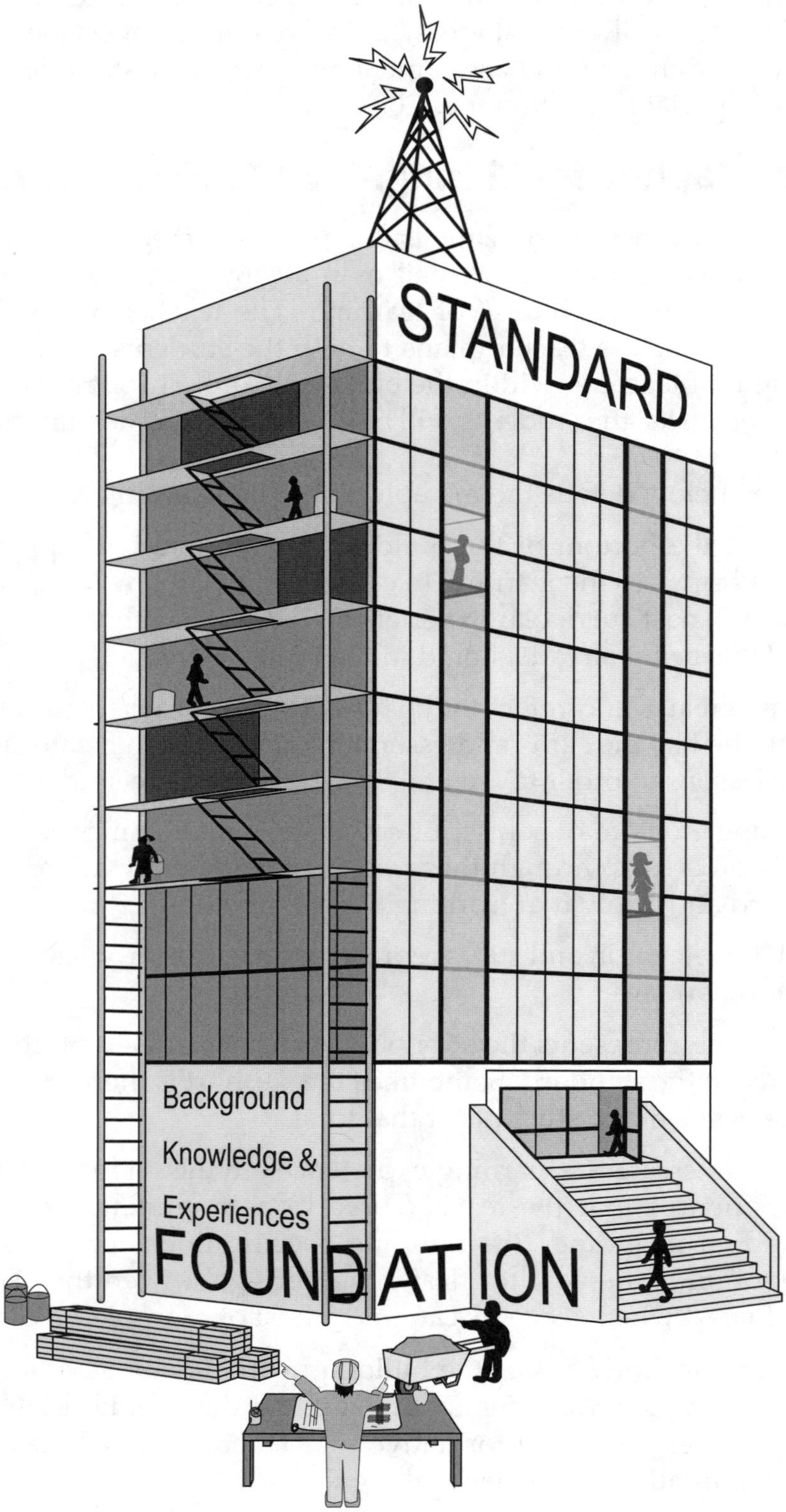

♦ Approaching the top of the building are the learning standards that we want every student to reach.

♦ At the top of the building is the transmission tower, which represents the enduring knowledge and understanding that can be transmitted and transferred to new situations and new ideas.

Just as in constructing a building, constructing a tiered lesson takes advanced planning. Thought must be given to scheduling, materials, timing and other logistics. The idea behind "The Learning Zone" is that learning isn't something you can "give"; it must be constructed by the students.

Research to Support Tiering

Tiering has been discussed in the literature by many authors and the focus on differentiated instruction over the last number of years has brought it to the forefront. Some of this literature is summarized below, and supports the notion of tiering as a way to support different levels of student readiness for learning.

Zone of Proximal Development (Vygotsky, Rieber, and Carton)

The Zone of Proximal Development (ZPD) is the zone in which learning occurs. Because the zone is different for students, they need to be working at different levels. The Zone of Actual Development (ZAD) is the area in which the student works independently with no help. Because the student has mastered the task, learning is not likely to occur within this zone. The learning is already accomplished, and the student is ready to move on.

Vygotsky, Rieber, and Carton (1988), say that if students who have similar ZPDs are grouped to work on the same skill or objective, teachers can design tasks to optimize learning by having the students accomplish a goal cooperatively. On the other hand, students placed in a group to do work that is outside their ZPD will be unable to accomplish the learning task even though they have the assistance of others in the group. Frustration occurs when students work outside of their ZPD.

Brain researchers explain that "learning occurs when the student experiences neither boredom nor anxiety—when he or she is neither over-challenged nor under-challenged" (Tomlinson, 2001).

Implications for Differentiation

♦ Pretesting is used to determine a student's ZPD for a particular objective, concept, or standard.

♦ When differentiating based on a child's readiness, place students in similar groups according to their readiness levels for a particular skill so frustration will not occur. These groups, however, should be re-formed frequently.

♦ The teacher should scaffold or support each learner in moving through tasks.

The Effects of Challenge on the Brain (Jensen, Jacobs, and Diamond)

Research found that graduate students' brains had 40% more neural connections than the brains of high school dropout students. Furthermore, graduates who had been involved in challenging activities showed more than 25% greater overall brain growth than the control group. Challenge and feedback were found to be two critical ingredients for maximizing brain growth (Jacobs, Schall, & Scheibel, 1993).

Diamond and Hopson, in their book, *Magic Trees of the Mind* (1998), say that dendrites on the neurons extend when the brain is in an enriched environment. Their research with rats found that an enriched environment is comprised of socialization and challenge. Rats within an impoverished environment actually had shrinkage of neural cell bodies and dendrites.

According to Jensen (2008), "To maximize learning, there's an edge we all should strive to maintain in our learners. The edge is a delicate balance between 'too easy' and 'not doable.' But it also must be relevant and meaningful. When we manage the learning variables in that 'zone of enrichment,' students feel excited and fulfilled. The brain is being enriched."

Implications for Differentiation

♦ If a student has already mastered an objective or skill, encourage and support that student as he/she moves to work on a more challenging task.

♦ When in doubt, teach up. The brain grows when challenged.

♦ Too much challenge—the students become frustrated and may quit.

♦ Too little challenge—the students become bored.

♦ Provide frequent check-in points to allow for feedback and adjustments of assignments.

Applying Tiered Objectives with Gifted Talented Children (Kettler and Curliss)

Kettler and Curliss (2003) review what current research reveals about mathematics instruction in a mixed-ability classroom with gifted learners. They conclude that differences in readiness are particularly significant in mathematics, and to attain optimal levels of learning for all students, teachers must modify the depth and complexity of concepts, as well as the pace of instruction. Using tiered lessons provides a framework for teachers so they can maximize learning for all students.

Implications for Differentiation

♦ Tiered instruction can help to support gifted learners in the "regular" classroom.

- The depth and complexity of concepts must be the focus of planning for tiering.
- The pace of instruction can be varied to provide extra support and challenge.

Middle School Tiering (Richards and Omdal)

The study by Richards and Omdal (2007) showed a significant difference between the scores of low background knowledge learners who experienced tiered instruction and low background learners who did not receive tiered instruction. The authors hypothesize that tiered instruction may be especially beneficial for struggling students. The authors emphasize the importance of professional development support for teachers and an understanding of the change process.

Implications for Differentiation

- Tiering is beneficial to all, but can be particularly helpful for struggling learners.
- Professional development is a crucial component in helping teachers learn how to effectively tier instruction.

Tiering Instruction Using a Common Outcome (Witherell and McMackin)

Witherell and McMackin (2002) propose that teachers must continually assess student learning. Their study had teachers use tiered graphic organizers as a way to formatively assess student learning. They have not yet conducted empirical studies, but have found through informal observation that leveled graphic organizers are one way to support a wide range of student understanding of concepts. The organizers are designed to focus on an important concept (e.g., compare and contrast, drawing conclusions) that the teacher uses as a whole-class lesson first. To assess student understanding of the concept, three levels of graphic organizers are used for learners who may need extra support or prompts for divergent thinking or increased complexity.

Implications for Differentiation

- Whole-class instruction can help the teacher "set the stage" for an important concept.
- Leveled graphic organizers for processing can be used to tier instruction and assess student learning.
- Lesson materials such as these can be used as springboards to proactively plan for differentiation for specific groups of learners.

Tying Things Together

This chapter provides information on what tiering is and isn't and synthesizes some of the research that supports the value of differentiating in this way. It compares tiering to the complexities of a construction zone. Chapter 2 will discuss how to celebrate individual differences, as well as provide practical ideas about how to group students for instruction and ways to communicate about differentiating instruction with parents.

For Further Reflection

♦ What new information have I added to my understanding of differentiated instruction?

♦ In what ways have I already tiered instruction?

♦ What personal experiences have I had that would confirm or refute the research discussed?

2

The Essential Building Blocks: Getting Ready to Tier

There is no harmony when everybody sings the same note.

—Doug Floyd

Once the foundation is created, we can begin to construct the frame of a structure using appropriate kinds of building material. Just as it takes a variety of people to successfully construct an architectural wonder, it also takes a variety of tools and creativity to design successful learning for all children. Although students have different ways of gaining new skills and content, and learn at different rates, they also have unique strengths, talents, and gifts that will support and encourage others. In the work world, companies are built on the diversity and collaboration found within their workforce. People want to be appreciated, respected and honored for their unique abilities. The following activities provide ideas about how to build a positive, collaborative classroom climate.

Activities That Celebrate Strengths and Encourage Growth

Ask Me Poster

This activity helps students focus on their own unique characteristics while giving them opportunities to collaborate with other students who may be able to help them when they are faced with a challenge.

Start with a class discussion and/or a story about being unique.

Have students sit in pairs or triads to brainstorm and discuss what they feel are their individual strengths.

- ♦ Create an "Ask Me!" poster that has a place for student names and have them write areas in which they have strength, and for which they may be able to offer help to others. (Figure 2.1).

- ♦ Post in a prominent place in the classroom, so students know who they might be able to ask for assistance when they encounter difficulties with particular tasks.

- ♦ Encourage students to add to their list of strengths as they grow and develop throughout the school year.

Figure 2.1. Ask Me! Poster

Ask Me!

Brittany	spelling and reading words, thinking of descriptive words, brainstorming ideas
Brock	organization, humor, following instructions, asking questions
Keaton	solving math problems, spelling, organizing writing
Aubrey	drawing, poetry, reading difficult words, being curious

Uniqueness Bingo

♦ Begin with a class discussion and/or a story or song about what makes each of us unique.

♦ Have students sit with partners or in triads to brainstorm and discuss ways they are unique and the special skills they have.

♦ Each student picks one unique trait to use for the game. Students circulate and complete bingo cards (Figure 2.2, Blackline Master 1) by asking other classmates to write their names and the unique trait they chose in one of the squares on their bingo board. Each square must be completed by a different classmate.

♦ Students return to their seats and the teacher sets up a game of "Uniqueness Bingo" by stating how a "bingo" will be won (e.g., horizontal/vertical line, four corners).

♦ The teacher randomly draws names and asks students to tell the one unique trait they chose to write about themselves on the bingo cards. If students have that student's name on their card, they place a marker on the square.

♦ Students call "bingo" when they have the required number and pattern of spaces required.

♦ The bingo cards could be posted in the room to remind students of the diversity of talents within the room or be kept for a free time activity.

Figure 2.2. Uniqueness Bingo!

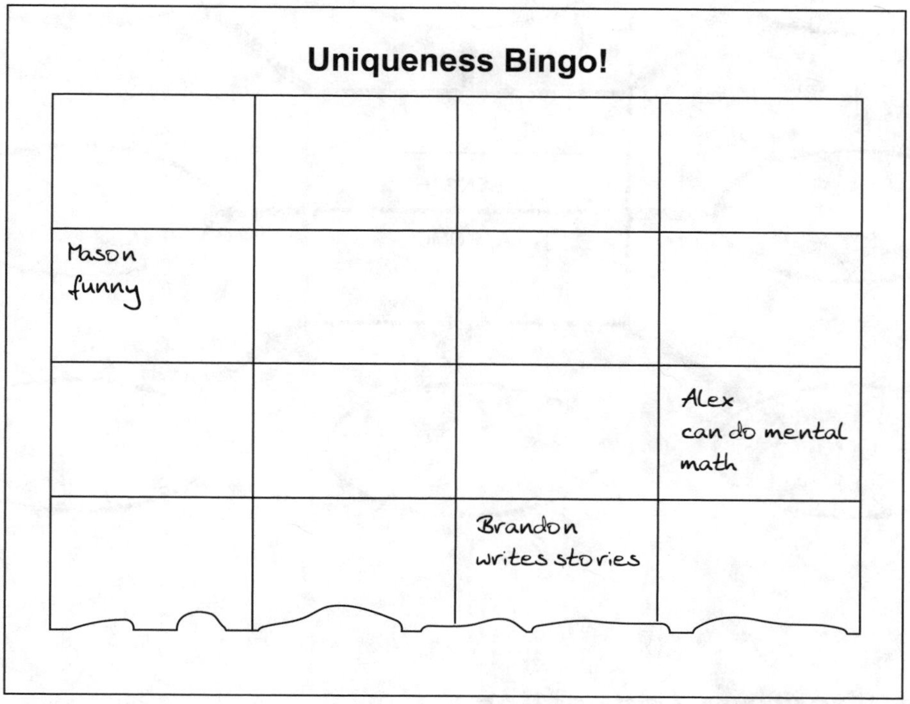

Uniqueness Bingo!

Mason funny			
			Alex can do mental math
		Brandon writes stories	

My Strengths Web

♦ Create a web that describes some of your personal strengths both at school and at home (Figure 2.3 is an example). Blackline Masters 2a and 2b provide templates that can be used.

♦ Discuss with students that everyone has strengths in different areas, and share your web.

♦ Ask students to examine their lives at home and school. Have them complete the following two web posters: My Strengths at School and My Strengths at Home, listing specific examples about their strengths. For example, "I love cooperative learning opportunities and am good at playing board games with friends and family."

♦ Display these web posters in the hallway or classroom for all to see and celebrate the diversity of strengths within the classroom. They can also be used to find classroom experts on certain topics or with particular skills.

Figure 2.3. My Strengths Web

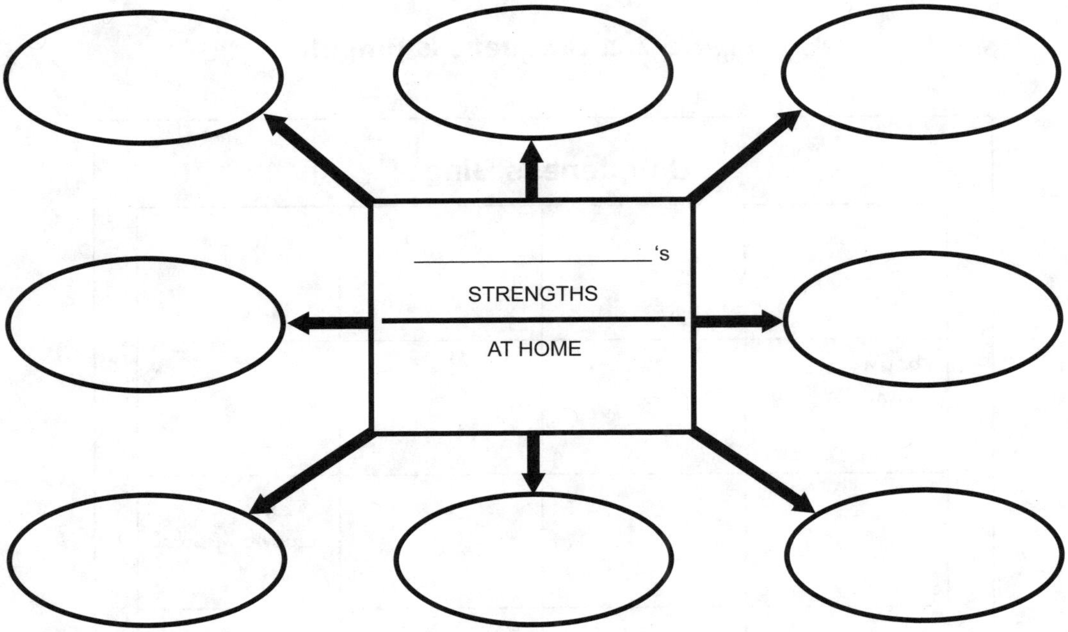

A web diagram with a central box labeled "_____'s STRENGTHS AT HOME" with arrows pointing outward to eight empty ovals.

Children's Literature Connections

Well-chosen books are excellent teaching tools. Stories are a wonderful way to celebrate individual strengths and uniqueness, and there are many titles that can help to build a positive classroom climate that supports differentiation. Some suggested titles are listed below, including both picture books and novels.

- ◆ Books to Celebrate Personal Gifts
  - *Ish* – Peter Reynolds
  - *Giraffes Can't Dance* – Gilles Andrae
  - *The Dot* – Peter Reynolds
  - *The Important Book* – Margaret Wise Brown
  - *Some Dogs Do* – Jez Alborough
  - *Frederick* – Leo Lionni
  - *Freak The Mighty* – Rodman Philbrick
  - *The Contender* – Robert Lipsyte

- ◆ Books About Individuality
  - *Leo, the Late Bloomer* – Robert Kraus
  - *Wanda and the Wild Hair* – Barbara Azore
  - *The Mixed Up Chameleon* – Eric Carle
  - *The Skin You Live In* – Michael Tyler
  - *Mrs. Spitzer's Garden* – Edith Pattou
  - *Olga the Brolga* – Rod Clement
  - *A Color of His Own* – Leo Lionni
  - *Incredible Me* – Kathi Appelt
  - *Unique Monique* – Maria Rousaki
  - *Travel Team* – Mike Lupica
  - *Blubber* – Judy Blume
  - *Stargirl* – Jerry Spinelli
- ◆ Books About Diversity
  - *Hooray for You!* – Marianne Richmond
  - *A Rainbow of Friends* – P.K. Hallinan
  - *No Two Snowflakes* – Shere Fitch
  - *All the Colors of the Earth* – Sheila Hammanaka
  - *We All Sing With the Same Voice* – Philip Miller
  - *We Are All Related—A Celebration of our Cultural Heritage* – students of G.T. Cunningham Elementary School
  - *Just Because I Am: A Child's Book of Affirmation* – Lauren Murphy Payne
  - *I Like Me* – Nancy Carlson
  - *Sister Anne's Hands* – Marybeth Lorbiecki
  - *A Friendship for Today* – Patricia McKissack
- ◆ Books About Acceptance
  - *Stand Tall, Molly Lou Melon* – Patty Lovell
  - *The Keeping Quilt* – Patricia Polacco
  - *The Rainbow Fish* – Marcus Pfister
  - *Whoever You Are* – Mem Fox
  - *The Table Where Rich People Sit* – Byrd Baylor
  - *Seven Blind Mice* – Ed Young

- *Peach and Blue* – Sarah S. Kilbourne
- *A Rainbow of Friends* – P.K. Hallinan
- *The Man Who Loved Clowns* – Dowell
- *Hundred Dresses* – Eleanor Estes
- *Rules* – Bynthia Lord
- *Boy in the Striped Pajamas* – John Boyne
- *Loser* – Jerry Spinelli
- *The Monument* – Gary Paulsen
- *Fame and Glory in Freedom, Georgia* – Barbara O'Connor

Grouping and Tiered Instruction

In a differentiated classroom, it is important that groups are not stagnant. There are several structures or combinations of structures that can be used for flexible grouping.

Figure 2.4. The Organization of Flexible Groups

Group Structure	Examples of How to Create Groups	Task Examples
Random Group	Draw names, count off numbers, matching puzzle pieces, use decks of cards	Process new content, social activities, field trip groups
Interest Group	Interest surveys and inventories, student sign-up at unit start	Access new content connected to standard through interests and choice
Readiness Group	Preassessment tasks, standardized assessment (e.g., Diagnostic Reading Assessment [DRA]), formative assessments, observation, etc.	Reteaching or new strategy teaching for those students needing additional processing or those who may need to work in more depth or complexity
Cooperative Learning Group	Interest, learning profile, or choice based	A task that requires explicit roles and responsibilities for each member within the group for the task to be completed (e.g., literature circles)
Independent Studies	Preassessment, student choice assignments, teacher-assigned tasks per student	Project choice boards, curriculum-compacted assignments, learning contracts

In tiered instruction, however, the groups are not created by interest, or learning profile, nor are they random. Tiered instruction is related to student readiness, and teachers must conduct a preassessment to determine students' understanding of a concept, which then determines how students will be grouped. The initial assessment, or preassessment, can be a comprehensive pre-assessment which covers all of the objectives from the unit, or an individual, small chunk pre-assessment focused on the upcoming lesson/objectives. In a differentiated classroom, placing students in small groups based on readiness levels is just one of many ways in which students may be grouped for instruction. Chapter 3 provides more information about preassessment.

Cooperative Learning

Students will, at times, work in groups during tiered instruction. Group work can present a challenge, but having structure and purpose can help. Cooperative learning strategies can be helpful and have been shown to be effective in supporting student learning.

- Research from Marzano, Pickering, and Pollock (2001) describes a 27 percentile gain in retention of content when students are placed into cooperative groups to learn/process information.

- Our brains were designed with the need to interact with others. The school social environment is changing the physical structure of children's brains.

- Research suggests that an increase in social support lowers blood pressure in hypertensive subjects (Uchino, Cacioppo, & Kiecolt-Glaser, 1996) and improves the immune system (Padgett, MacCallum, & Sheridan, 1998).

- Eric Jensen (2005) suggests that "students should spend 5–20% of class time in social groupings, and grouping should be used purposefully and strategically."

Cooperative learning strategies can be grouped into the following categories: strategies to use before students are grouped, while they are grouped, and after the group work has been accomplished.

Before Grouping Strategies

- Know what the essential question or the enduring understanding is regarding the unit of study. Choose the standard, objective, or chunk of learning that this task will support. Write out clearly what you want the students to be able to know, understand and be able to do. What will learning look and sound like?

- Brainstorm activities that will meet the needs of students. For example, think about adjustments of support, open-endedness, and complexity. Ensure all learners will reach the standard with equally engaging tasks (several ideas for adjusting the activities can be found in Figure 4.4, page 53).

- Create a list of rules that the students need to follow during group time. Ask your students to help develop this list. For example they might come up with "respect and responsibility." They must show each member respect (brainstorm what respect *looks like* and *sounds like* during a group activity), and they must be responsible throughout the group activity. These lists could be turned into a rubric or checklist to ensure that the rules are being followed during the group time. A poster template can be found on Blackline Master 6.

- As the tasks are designed for the groups, gather the materials necessary to complete the task so that you will have a model to use in your teaching. With the materials in hand, visualize the task and ask yourself, "What steps will students need to follow? What might the students do with the directions and the materials that I don't want them to do?" With this knowledge in mind, clearly set your expectations for the tasks.

- Write a sequential list of instructions for each of the tasks so that each group gets a personalized list of directions for the specific task at hand. Use as few words as possible. For example: "1. Group the items into at least three different categories. 2. Create a label for each group using the sticky notes." The sticky notes, a pen, and the items would be included in a task envelope. (See Blackline Master 4 for a reproducible Task Assignment Details.) Describe how the students will know when the task is completed, where they are to place the product of this work when they are done, and what they should do with any remaining time.

- Provide a list of "Must Do" and "May Do" tasks so there is a clear order of tasks to be completed, and a short list of choices for those who finish early (Blackline Master 5).

- Provide a rubric (checklist, analytical, or holistic) that displays the criteria and performance standards for the work to be accomplished. Decide if it will be completed by the group and its members or completed as a class after the task is complete. Make sure the students know exactly how they will be evaluated on the task; go over the whole rubric or checklist to make sure they all understand. (Websites like www.rubrics4teachers.com and www.rubistar.4teachers.org can help you create your rubric.)

- Use a poster or white board to write general directions during group time so that students can reference it, if necessary. Some things to include might be the group rules, the goal of the group activity, time allotment, where to turn in the work, a reminder to complete group evaluation, and what to do when the group goal has been accomplished. (See Blackline Master 6 for the Group Work Expectation Poster.)

- Group Role Cards could be explained and distributed. Consider limiting the number of roles within a group at the beginning of the year until students understand each role clearly. It is also important to give students experience throughout the year with all of the different roles. Blackline Masters 7 and 8 contain sets of role cards, one that is graphic and most suitable for younger learners (Figure 2.5), and another more suitable for older learners (Figure 2.6). They can be reproduced and given to students as a reminder of what their role in the group will be. They can also be changed to meet your individual group of learners. A learning contract can be used in a similar fashion (see Blackline Master 9, the Learning Contract Group Work). This is not an exhaustive list of possible roles, just a starting point.

During Group Work Strategies

Teach, model, and practice how to get help when needed. Students can often get help from other students. Raising hands is often ineffective, because the teacher is usually engrossed in working with another group of students that need him/her. Encourage students to ask others for help in other effective ways:

♦ *Ask Three Before Me:* Students are to ask three other students the question before asking the teacher for help.

♦ *Question Board:* Create a "Question Board" where students are to place a sticky note with the questions that arise. The teacher will gather the notes and circulate as required or stop to discuss with the whole class when appropriate.

♦ *"Please Help" Tent Cards:* Students create "Please Help" tent cards on their tables (only one per table is needed.) On one side of the tent card are the words "Please Help," while on the opposite side are the words "Keep Working." When a student has exhausted all avenues of help at his table or beyond, the student takes the "Please Help" tent and sets it up on the table so that the teacher can see the "Please Help" side. The "Keep Working" side is a reminder to the students that they must continue working until the teacher is free to come and help (Blackline Master 10).

♦ *Green/Yellow/Red Stacking Cups:* Students are given green, red, and yellow cups that stack. If the green is on the top of the stack it signifies to the teacher that the student is working well, without difficulty. Yellow on the top of the stack signifies they are beginning to have trouble, but can still continue. A red cup on top means that they cannot continue their work without help.

♦ Teach, model, and practice the conversation noise levels you expect during work times. A "partner-talk" level of conversation is appropriate. That means that two people can talk in a low voice (not a whisper) and hear one another without hearing two others at the same table. It takes practice, but the entire class can do partner-talk together and the room has a good, busy buzz going on. Consider creating a poster of a traffic light. Place a pointer or clothes pin on the green light if their voices are at an appropriate level. Place the pointer on yellow if they should be conscious of turning the volume down. Place the pointer on red if all voices need to be off for further instructions (see Blackline Master 11).

♦ Teach, model, and practice when, where, and how students are to move during group time. For example, how are students to get materials or hand in their work?

♦ Play soft music in the background to help block out extraneous noise. Research suggests the music can act like a wall so that other groups aren't distracted by the talk of the other groups (Restak, 2002).

♦ If you need to briefly stop the groups while they are working, raise a hand and say "News Flash." Give instructions, but speak quickly so the students can get back to work. Cognitively, students can do one thing at a time. They'll be able to listen to you or work on their assignments, but not both simultaneously.

♦ Consider the use of other signals such as train whistles or chimes.

After Grouping Strategies

♦ After every cooperative learning experience, students should take time to reflect and determine how they can improve the next time and to praise one another for a good job. They evaluate whether or not they fulfilled their role, stayed on task, encouraged and listened to one another, and accomplished the goal (see Blackline Masters 12 and 13 for examples).

♦ When the group work is completed, bring the class together to debrief the work and bring closure to the learning.

♦ Take time to reflect on whether or not the students were placed in the best group for their personal success. Ask yourself:

• Were the students on task? If not, what hindered them from staying more on task (noise in the room, unclear directions, roles not defined properly, too challenging or not challenging enough)?

• Did the students accomplish the assigned objective? Why or why not?

• Did you provide appropriate materials, directions, time allotment, and group dynamics?

• What steps do I need to take now? Reteach? Reinforce with different elaboration techniques? Explain the group rules better?

Bringing Parents On Board

Parents are a vital part to a successful differentiated classroom. From the first open house through parent–teacher–student conferences, we must share our beliefs and practices for teaching and learning. Parents need to feel confident that their children are being appropriately challenged. We must take the time to show them the standards and how we intend to meet them through readiness, interest and learning profiles and describe what supports are in place to help if difficulties arise. Each child will get what is fair for them and will continue to move ahead in their learning. Differentiation helps us to accomplish these goals.

We recommend that you share the following concepts with parents to help them understand that you are only doing this for their child's benefit.

♦ Research to support tiering

♦ When you might be tiering lessons and why you choose to tier

♦ Flexibility of the groupings (i.e., they are not permanent)

Tying Things Together

This chapter discusses some of the ways teachers can celebrate individual strengths while helping students develop skills to function effectively during both group and independent work. Chapter 3 will provide steps for setting up successful tiered lessons in the classroom.

For Further Reflection

♦ How do I celebrate individual student strengths?

♦ How do I group students and what strategies do I use to ensure group work is effective and productive?

♦ How do I communicate how I differentiate instruction with my parent group?

3

The Blueprint for Tiering: Designing with the End in Mind

If we did all the things we are capable of doing, we would truly astound ourselves.

—Thomas Edison

As the building continues, there is continual reference to the blueprints. They are created before construction begins, and are drawn with the vision of the completed structure in mind. Similarly, there must be an end goal in mind when tiering instruction, as well as constant checks to ensure the learning goal is achieved. For effective student learning, we must consider when it might be important to tier instruction and what assessment we will use to determine how instruction could be tiered.

When to Tier

Starting at the beginning of the year it is wise to give students varied activities that are not necessarily based on ability, interest, or even learning profile. Why? So that students can see that we can all get to the same objective in a variety of ways, and through those different pathways we may all bring a different perspective to the learning. In this way, they will be exposed early to the concept that you will be giving different assignments to different students—that students will get the tasks that will help them move forward in their learning.

When tiering actually begins to happen in your classroom, it needs no name. Groups that are flexible and together for short periods of time do not need to be labeled as, for example, the Bluebirds and Redbirds. Our goal as educators is to help all students reach the same learning destination, but some will do it through using extra supports and others by thinking in more depth or complexity.

In addition, tiering is only one way of differentiating, and as such is used only when necessary to move students forward in their knowledge and skills. A variety of assistance and support, the quantity and complexity of resources, and the varying levels of process and product make student success more likely.

It may be helpful to keep track of when you differentiate by readiness (tier) as well as when you differentiate in other ways (e.g., by interest and learning preference). Figure 3.1 and Blackline Master 14 contains a table that can be used over a period of time to ensure that tiering is balanced with other methods of differentiation. It could also be used to track differentiation within a unit plan or as a reflection tool to determine how much differentiating is occurring over time. Teachers can jot down a note about the lesson, or simply shade or place a check mark in the squares to indicate how lessons were differentiated, and in what way.

Figure 3.1. Balancing Ways of Differentiating

Jot down a note about lessons, or simply shade or place a check mark in the squares to indicate how lessons were differentiated, and in what way.

Readiness	Interest	Learning Profile
Tiered spelling lesson	Fractions with chocolate bars in math	Learning strength groups in math
Tiered cubes for science project	Health WebQuest	Multiple intelligences tic-tac-toe in reading
Guided reading	Social studies RAFT	Learning preferences choices for music project

So how do you know when to tier and when to do other types of differentiation? This checklist may help in your decision as to whether you will tier or not. If you check one or more of the boxes, it might be a good idea to consider tiering the lesson.

☐ After your preassessment, you notice that some students need more background knowledge, basic skills, and more time before the standard can be reached.

☐ After your preassessment, you notice that some students have already mastered the objective.

☐ Having taught the concept in previous years, you know that teaching this standard brings challenges.

☐ Your teacher instincts or knowledge about a particular class of students leads you to believe that students will be more successful if you have students doing different kinds of work.

How to Set Up Tiering

Study Your Standards

The very first place to start when planning to tier is with the required standards. The standards are guidelines that show what a student must be able to know, understand, and be able to do. Some important standards are framed with "essential questions," or "big ideas," or "enduring understanding" (Wiggins & McTighe, 2005). Within the tiered lesson plan, teachers should write out what The Big Picture is for the whole lesson. The following sequence may clarify the appropriate standards and allow for a variety of strategies to use for your students.

♦ Write your standards out for the particular unit (these are usually big picture and general). Your district will provide you with the state and district standards.

♦ List the specific objectives that will help the students achieve mastery of the standard for the entire unit in the following categories: Students will know, understand, and be able to do (KUDo).

Now you are ready for the next step which is brainstorming potential assessments that may be used during the unit so that you can create the preassessment pieces.

Brainstorm Assessments and Implement Preassessments

Assessment is one of the cornerstones of good instruction. Good assessment is simply using appropriate tools to gather and review data on student learning. The commonly used assessments include closed-response tasks such as true/false items, multiple-choice selection, fill-in-the-blank with and without word banks, and matching. Other tools that could be used include open-response items such as written response, analogies, drawings, reflections, projects, and presentations.

After studying your objectives, create a list of potential assessments that could be used within your teaching unit (e.g., water-cycle vocabulary quiz, water-cycle diagram, word web or mind map, meteorology report using vocabulary words, writing daily weather updates).

The following questions will help you create the list of assessments:

♦ What will your summative assessment(s) look like based on the standards for this unit?

♦ What is the need-to-know information?

♦ How can I best discover what my students know about this information?

♦ Will a performance task represent the learning better than an open response task?

♦ Will closed responses get to the heart of some deeper content issues?

♦ Will I observe?

♦ Will I take anecdotal notes?

♦ How will I include student self-assessment?

♦ What tools will I use and at what points in the learning?

Preassessments are now chosen from these assessments. Preassessments are small chunks of assessments that you plan to use during the unit, so there is enough time to adjust instruction. There are several different types of preassessments that you might want to consider using.

Types of Preassessments

Comprehensive Preassessment

A comprehensive preassessment can be given prior to the introduction of a new unit of study to determine if tiering is necessary and if so, what tiers are necessary to facilitate learning. Comprehensive assessment addresses more of an overview of knowledge and can even include a student's self-assessment (Gareis & Grant, 2008). An example of this type of preassessment is having students brainstorm words that they associate with the upcoming topic. If students are able to list a number of strong vocabulary words related to the topic, the teacher might decide to give those few students a more in-depth question or interview the students to determine if there is strong understanding of concepts and skills. Another comprehensive preassessment of this type would be to simply ask students to write down or discuss what they know about an upcoming unit. This can give the teacher a sense of which students have a great deal of background knowledge and which students may need extra support.

Focused Preassessment

The focused preassessment checks for understanding of every objective within the upcoming unit. This is designed by creating questions that correspond with objectives within the unit. This could include multiple-choice, true false, or open-ended response questions. Teachers could also use parts of an end-of-the-chapter test or a preassessment from a textbook.

There are pros and cons to a focused preassessment. *The pros:* You can see background knowledge of the students from a unit perspective. This could provide information about where to begin the teaching, which objectives to skip because all students have it mastered, or which objectives might need more time. Both teachers and students can see the growth at the conclusion of the unit when preassessment results are compared to postassessment results.

The cons: A focused preassessment over a unit does take longer to administer and grade than some other preassessments, but let us challenge you with this thought: Priming is a very important instructional strategy in that it gives the brain a preview of what is coming up. Neural networks in the brain are established and highlighted before the unit instruction actually occurs. This could improve learning connections since there is existing background knowledge before the unit begins. Focused preassessments are great examples of priming the brain, especially when you take the time to review the answers with the students as they self-correct their papers.

If the focused unit preassessment doesn't sound too inviting to you, then this next category may sound "just right." This is where you take a small section or objective from the unit you are about to teach, and only preassess that small chunk. These quick, easy, yet still focused preassessments only take a couple of minutes to create and administer. They include true or false, matching, cloze activities, definitions of words, or the 5 Ws (who, what, where, when, why or how).

Formative Assessments as In-Route Check Points

With differentiation there is always positive intent, which is one quality that makes differentiation better than just using a "best practice" strategy. With each student in mind, the teacher intentionally chooses the preassessments and formative assessments that will support student learning.

As the unit of study proceeds, assessment continues in an ongoing manner. This formative assessment might match the preassessment given before the unit began, but it may be different. It allows the teacher to take quick checks along the way to see if the students have caught on to a particular skill or understand a specific concept. It is from these formative assessments that decisions are made on whether specific content or a skill needs to be retaught in a new way or given additional practice time, and that decisions are made for forming new flexible groups for reteaching purposes.

The following examples can be used for both preassessment and formative assessment as quick ways to gather data and determine where in the learning students are in their understanding based on the standards. After choosing and using a tool of assessment, the next step is to decide "What have I learned from this information?" and "What am I going to do for the students now?" Those two questions lead to the second part of our assessments which is the "So What, Now What?" section which can help you begin to think about the next steps.

Specific Examples of Preassessments and Formative Assessments

Understanding "So What, Now What?"

In every assessment that we design as teachers, we must have certain questions ready to ask and answer before we give the assessment and after the assessment has been administered. Without these questions and answers, the assessments are virtually invalid. The simple questions that need to be asked are:

♦ What information are you expecting to get from the assessment?

♦ What data did you get from this student (or group of students)?

♦ What does this information tell you?

♦ What are your next steps?

At the commencement of any unit of study, we have certain goals, objectives, and standards that we acknowledge will be taught in that unit. Our purpose in a preassessment is to see if any of our students already possess some background knowledge or even have fully developed skills and knowledge that meet the standards set by our district. With the first question we might expect to get a measure of knowledge based on what we know our school district has offered in the vertical curriculum (the grades and courses coming before the present course), but then we would assume that there is a natural stopping place for most of the students because that material would be what our course would be teaching.

The second question leads us to consider the actual data that we get from the assessment. If it's a preassessment, did we get more specific information about the knowledge and skills than what we would have expected? Was there a deeper level of understanding from some students that made us aware of the student's higher level of thinking or problem solving?

The information may lead us to consider giving a more in-depth preassessment to a particular student to see if the depth of knowledge is truly greater than usual or just a one-time fluke. Does the information tell us (if the assessment is formative) that a concept or skill needs to be retaught using a different strategy or does the student need more practice time?

Finally, the last question forces us to intently decide what we plan to do next. Do any students need to be involved in an independent study because the curriculum can use compacting? Do students need to be brought up to a more basic level of understanding even before the grade-level standards can be truly taught?

Using these four questions as we design and administer assessments, we will more likely choose assessments that address the standards and content that we consider the most important in answering essential questions.

ABC Brainstorm

Each student or small group of students in a class is assigned a different letter of the alphabet and they must select a word starting with that letter that is related to the topic being studied. Alternatively, the students could list as many words as possible related to the given topic from A to Z (see Blackline Master 3). It is a good way to prime the brain when starting a unit of study or to see how vocabulary is developing during the course of a unit of study.

So What, Now What? If students are able to list a number of strong vocabulary words related to the topic, the teacher might decide to give those few students a more in depth preassessment to see what the stronger students actually know, or the teacher might just interview the students first to see if there is strong understanding of concepts and skills that would indicate the need for adjusting assignments. As a formative assessment the ABC Brainstorm may be done at various times during the course of the unit to give students additional opportunities to reinforce key vocabulary. The more practice they give to this categorizing the easier it is for them to access the words when they need them.

Anticipation Guide

A checklist is written to activate prior knowledge and evaluate what a student knows before the lesson and then used to reflect upon what has been learned (Figure 3.2, Blackline Master 15). Before the lesson, students read each statement and mark whether they agree or disagree. Next, they participate in the lesson and then re-read the statements and mark whether they still agree or disagree with the statement based on what they learned. They should be ready to support new beliefs with evidence from the lesson by jotting ideas after "Support It."

Figure 3.2. Anticipation Guide

Agree	Disagree		Agree	Disagree
√		1. Fungi must form spores to reproduce. **Support It:**		√
	√	2. All mushrooms are safe for us to eat. **Support It:**	√	
√		3. Yeast is a form of fungus. **Support It:**	√	
√		4. Penicillin is made by a fungus. **Support It:**	√	

So What, Now What? An anticipation guide gives each student an opportunity to reflect on what is known before and after the learning experience. During this general assessment, observe the responses of the students and record anecdotal notes of any significance. Although results of this assessment may indicate that the majority of the students within the class have some understanding, the teacher can begin to move ahead with the new content and teaching, the anticipation guide sometimes triggers more interest in the upcoming content ideas.

Closed Response Items

Closed response items such as multiple choice, true/false, and fill-in-the-blank with a word bank are appropriate ways to assess content and skill in some situations. Because many standardized tests also use multiple choice items with a stem (the question or statement), the answer, and several distractors, students need instruction on how to respond to these types of assessments. Richard J. Stiggins explains in *Student-Centered Classroom Assessment* (2000) that students can master content in many ways, including memorization, repetition of experiences, and reasoning out a proposition or sequence. He also says, "Useable knowledge takes many forms, including facts, concepts, principles or generalizations, and procedures." He adds "[s]killful selected response test items" will tap into student mastery of this knowledge (p. 119).

So What, Now What? Closed response items can help assess mastery of understanding of the standards for a unit of study, as well as some procedural knowledge that supports skills within a content area, and even student attitude, values, and other affective states. Do students need reteaching on particular parts of the standard? Can the teacher have the student redo or respond in a different way to those items missed on the closed response quiz?

Door Pass

The "Door Pass" (Blackline Master 16) is an effective way to formatively assess student understanding of concepts and skill to determine where students need additional clarification or assistance. They are also useful to stimulate critical thinking and as a springboard to link new learning with existing knowledge. Usually the questions are designed to be answered during the first or last few minutes of class. If the Door Pass is given out at the end of class most immediately after the initial teaching, keep in mind that the responses sometimes are those of short-term memory. When the Door Passes are offered as assessment at the beginning of the following day's class, the students have had a night's sleep where the brain has started the task of consolidating the learning and is working to take it to long-term memory.

Examples of Door Pass questions:

- ♦ Draw and/or explain two ways that materials in the home are recycled.
- ♦ Solve for x: $2(3x - 7) + 4(3x + 2) = 6(5x + 9) + 3$
- ♦ Using a T-chart, compare and contrast mitosis and meiosis.

So What, Now What? After the Door Pass slips are turned in, flip through them, separating the correct from the incorrect responses. If the responses are correct, then the instruction was on the mark and can continue as it is. If there are a few students who did not get the correct answers, they can be retaught in a small group. If the majority of the answers are incorrect, you are alerted that the students are still confused and the concept should be taught using a different strategy and may need more time to be processed.

H-Diagram

The H-Diagram is a formative assessment and/or processing tool in the shape of an H that is used to link two items by their attributes and/or characteristics of items (things, people, places, ideas, etc.). A taped H on the floor using actual items can be used for a kinesthetic demonstration, or a simple drawing on a large laminated poster board can be used so students can write or draw their responses.

The topics are written on slips of paper and placed at the top of the two columns of the H. Under each topic the student lists all the characteristics true of that item on slips of paper and lay them in the column. After everything is listed the students examine the characteristic on one side of the H and compare it to the list of the opposite side. If the two characteristics are similar, one of the slips with the characteristic is placed in the "similarities," or middle of the H and the other is discarded. If the characteristic does not have a match with the other item, it is left in its own column. The activity can also be done using a paper graphic organizer (Blackline Master 17).

Figure 3.3. H-Diagram

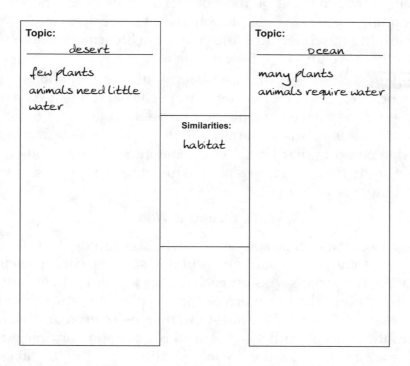

Topic:

____desert____

few plants
animals need little
water

Similarities:

habitat

Topic:

____ocean____

many plants
animals require water

So What, Now What? If students are unable to complete the H-Diagram and explain why certain descriptors belong with one item or the other, then students need to explore a variety of resources as partners or triads and process the information in one or more "comparative" graphic organizers with more intense teacher assistance.

Likert Scale or Line of Continuum

This is a type of survey where the students are asked to identify the degree with which they agree or disagree with a given statement. It can also be used to self-assess understanding of a particular concept, measure attitudes, preferences, and subjective reactions. Large number signs are hung on a wall or taped to the floor so that students can stand at the appropriate place on the continuum. After students have chosen their places, question students on their self-placement. Although it may take much modeling and practice, students should be able to provide comments and statements that support their reasons for making a particular choice. Students should also be encouraged to move, based on what other students offer in their statements, if they desire.

Here is an example of a survey question: Stand on the Likert Scale based on your understanding of rocks and minerals.

1   2   3   4   5   6

Students who have little background knowledge with science curriculum in this area would probably move to stand on the 1 or 2. If a student has a hobby of collecting rock specimens or going spelunking, the student might move up to the 3. A student who has both the background in school curriculum and the life experiences with rocks and minerals would likely move up to a 4, 5, or even a 6.

So What, Now What? Based on the discussion with the students as they support their self-assessment, decide whether or not any specific students need a private interview with you to see if they have a deeper and broader understanding of the concept. If the information the students share seems to be what you expected, and is typical for the basic knowledge entering that grade level/content area, then you can proceed to develop the unit of study based on the standards given, and adjust for more support or more complexity if there is a need.

W, W, W, W, and H Web

This web is best used as a formative assessment because students design better questions when they have some understanding and interest in the concept being explored. Divide the class into five groups. Assign each group a part of a concept web—who, what, where, when, or how. The key word or topic is placed in the center of a piece of paper. Each group brainstorms all of the questions that they can create that relate to their question word and the concept. Either the same day or at another time, groups switch boxes (e.g., the "how" group takes the "who" questions, the "who" takes the "what" questions, etc.). Each group tries to find as many answers as possible to the questions designed by the other group. Later, the original group gets its original questions with the answers from the other students. This "home" group then reviews the questions and answers and chooses its top two or three to present to the class as the ones that best represent the information. (See Blackline Master 18 for the template.)

So What, Now What? The majority of time during the two sessions is spent observing students as they work in cooperative groups to come up with good questions, and as they research and support the answers they are finding to the questions they must answer. The teacher may need to scaffold the questioning and the researching by supporting the work with guiding questions along the way. The guidelines for cooperative group should be followed and self-assessments for cooperative work are vital.

Levels of Knowing

This preassessment allows students to evaluate the level of knowledge they have about vocabulary words from literature or content area. It evaluates whether the student knows the word well, has some knowledge of the word, or has never seen or heard of the word. Choose four to six words to write in the "Words" column. Photocopy one per student. Read a contextual sentence with the first word in it. Ask the students to place a check mark in the appropriate column. If the student checks either of the columns "I know this word well" or" I recognize this word, but don't own it," the student should guess the meaning of the word in the appropriate column. If the student checks "I have no idea," the student does not need to guess the meaning. After all of the words have been read within the contextual sentence and students have placed their check marks in the appropriate places, definitions should be given for each word. (Allen & Nickelsen, 2008)

So What, Now What? Once you collect each student's Level of Knowing, you will be able to determine which words need more elaboration, which words require more time to learn, and the student's overall background knowledge on the terms they will encounter within that lesson, book, or unit. The bonus in this strategy is the jumpstart in teaching vocabulary terms by creating the simple definitions in the last column.

Assessment + Knowing Your Students = Differentiated Instruction

Not all students are successful at having their learning quantified through certain assessment formats. Some students are great at answering the closed responses and short-answer formats, whereas others are better at showing what they know through the open response or written response format. Many students are able to perform better when their learning is showcased over time in a growth portfolio, where there is a multitude of formats—videotapes, audiotapes, reflections, writings, drafts, published work, performance tasks, and journals. Still other students are able to represent their understanding and mastery through the presentations and project work that combines their synthesis of knowledge through the design of a research question, the research itself, and the work to showcase their findings. A true learning "portfolio" of a student would be a repertoire of assessment formats in each content area.

Now that you have written your standards and specific objectives, brainstormed assessments, and created preassessments for some objectives, it's time to choose the objectives that you believe need tiering. Remember to use the guidelines for when to tier (page 31) in making this decision. There is no set number of lessons that must be tiered within a unit. It all depends on your students' preassessment results and standards. Now, let's take the objectives that you believe might need to be tiered.

Brainstorm Ways to Support Students with the Chosen Objectives

Take one of the objectives that you will tier from the unit and brainstorm strategies that will help your students be successful with the objective. Some students might already have mastered that objective, so how can you enrich those students' understanding of the objective? If some students lack even the basic skills to allow them to work toward the grade-level objectives, strategies must be brainstormed that will build their understanding and skills to move closer to a level of basic knowledge. Now, study the preassessment results. Which strategy would be best for your groups of students? In Chapter 4, we show you how to write these strategies in an objective format, and from there create tiered lessons.

Tying Things Together

This chapter provides information about knowing when to tier instruction and recognizing that tiered instruction is only one way to differentiate instruction. It has also given some information about assessment and strategic grouping of students. Chapter 4 provides a lesson plan template and examples to help guide the planning process for tiering.

For Further Reflection

♦ How will I determine when it is necessary to tier instruction?

♦ What are my current methods of assessing student readiness? What new strategies can I incorporate into my practice?

♦ How do I plan for tiering?

4

Pour the Concrete!
It's Time to Tier

He who fails to plan, plans to fail.

—Author Unknown

Once the foundation is ready, the materials are assembled, the blueprint is at the forefront, and a plan is in place, it's time to begin building. One way to ensure a successful building is to study examples of completed projects and use them as a model that can guide new work. In this chapter, we discuss the steps to creating powerful, tiered lesson plans, along with many examples of tiered lessons and a planning template. The lesson examples are just that—suggestions that may help you build a picture of what tiered instruction can look like. In most cases, they are not meant to be copied and used because they may not meet your specific learning standards or what you discover about the needs of your students through preassessment. They may, however, be used as a springboard to help you develop tiered lessons to meet the needs of your individual group of learners.

Construction Specifications: The Tiered Lesson Plan Template

The Tiered Lesson Plan template (Figure 4.1, page 46) has been used in a variety of settings. It has been revised many times, yet is also open for your interpretation. It makes tiering easier for you as you begin to implement tiering and allows you to see how each group is being appropriately challenged.

The lesson plan structure incorporates the components of best practices and brain research. For example, research tells us that learning is all about connections—connecting new information to the background knowledge of each student. Identifying the "grabber and hook," for example, raises interest and helps students to activate their background knowledge so connections can be made. We also know that students learn best when they know what is expected of them, what they are going to learn, and how they are going to be assessed. The objective writing template helps to clarify these components.

From Unit to the Daily Lesson Plan

The Big Picture

Identify concepts, skills, essential questions, enduring knowledge, and/or the big standard that will be the focus of the unit. Now, write that big idea in the first box of the Tiered Lesson Plan Template (Blackline Master 19). You already have a list of the objectives that go along with this big idea or standard. These objectives are all related to the same theme or overall concept. Remember that objectives should have the specific content plus a verb (try to use higher level verbs using Bloom's or Anderson's Taxonomy). What exactly do you want your students to know, understand and be able to do?

Figure 4.1. Tiered Lesson Plan Template

The Big Picture of the Lesson: Concept, Skills, Essential Questions, Enduring Understandings or Standard	Preassessment	Materials
	Grabber & Hook	
	Instruction	

Basic Tier	Grade-Level Tier (START HERE)	Advanced Tier
The students will _____ *(Verb)* _____ *(Specific Content)* Assessment:	The students will _____ *(Verb)* _____ *(Specific Content)* Assessment:	The students will _____ *(Verb)* _____ *(Specific Content)* Assessment:

Closure:

As an example, the following objectives might be included in a social studies unit about the American Revolution:

Unit: American Revolution

The students will be able to:

♦ Explain the pros and cons of being a Loyalist or a Patriot.

♦ Use a graphic representation of some type to compare/contrast how Loyalists or Patriots would have felt during critical moments within the war.

♦ Diagram the progression of events leading to the American Revolution. Create a thesis statement about how the student would have done things differently if the student had been a Patriot or Loyalist during the American Revolution.

♦ Tell about one of the major events from this war. Use a cause-and-effect graphic organizer to explain the event.

♦ Choose one of the battles listed below. Create questions that need to be asked about that battle to discover its importance to the Revolution (e.g., What started this battle?). This will be completed as small-group jigsaws and shared with the whole class.

♦ Create a one-act play or Readers' Theater script about a moment in time from the American Revolutionary War. Include a famous person within the skit. Dramatize the events from their perspective.

Preassessment

Choose a method for preassessment, administer the tool, and gather the data to determine the prior knowledge of students for the new content, skills, and understanding that will be targeted for learning. This assessment should represent the key concepts/skills from each lesson that will be taught within the unit. Remember that preassessment comes from the assessments that give throughout the unit (formative and summative). Write this preassessment in the second box on The Tiered Lesson Plan Template.

Objectives

Put all of the objectives in a logical order for instruction according to the students' background knowledge, preassessment results, and materials available. You may need to adjust some objectives depending on the preassessment results. You may also want to consider which objectives may take more time for students to process, and which may take less.

Objective(s) to Spend More Time On:

♦ Explain the pros and cons of being a Loyalist or a Patriot.

Objective(s) to Spend Less Time On:

♦ Tell about one of the major events from this war.

Now that the objectives are in order, scrutinize the pretest results to see which lessons will need to be tiered. Remember, you don't need to tier every day, only when there is a need.

The results of the preassessment may compel you to make changes to your unit plan. Figure 4.2 describes some example of such adjustments:

Figure 4.2. Examples of Adjustments

Preassessment Result	Adjustment to Objective(s)
Mastery by all students	Change or delete the objective.
Nonmastery by all students	Make multiple content delivery options available and multiple processing opportunities available for whole-group teaching and assignments.
One group shows mastery and another shows nonmastery	Students who have mastered the objective(s) be given activities that will extend into higher level thinking or involve more complexity. The students who have not mastered the objectives will have different versions of a task for that particular objective, and have multiple content delivery options available. Multiple processing opportunities will also be made available for small-group teaching.
One group of students shows mastery, one group is approaching mastery, and one group shows nonmastery	Three different versions of a task will be created for that particular objective(s) with variations in complexity, thinking skills involved, and different kinds of support for small-group lessons and assignments.

Materials

Make sure to list all of the materials needed for each activity or tier so that all students will be successful. This list is helpful for proper preparation.

Grabber and Hook

To get the students fully involved in your lesson, you need to create a way to "grab" their attention. This section is usually creative, fun, and energizing. The purpose of the hook is to activate prior knowledge of the students so the new learning has something on which to "hook" or connect to.

Some ideas to "grab" their attention:

♦ Show an object related to the lesson

♦ Read a short picture book that intrigues them so they want to learn more

- Ask a challenging question
- Do a quick movement related to the concept (e.g., running in place before teaching about action verbs)
- Perform a quick experiment
- View a short video clip
- Listen to a song
- Play a game

Examples of More Detailed Grabbers and Hooks

- *Book Pass:* The teacher gives the students four to five minutes to examine a book—Table of Contents; its headings and subheadings; its pictures, photographs, diagrams, captions; and the book jacket. On their own "Book Pass" forms, students make notes that remind them about the book and what might interest them in returning to it at a later time or how they might interest a classmate in the resource. After giving the students the time for the review and note-taking, the teacher calls "Pass" and the students begin passing the books around the classroom tables or rows until the teacher says, "Stop and review." At that time, the student begins the process with a new resource. This continues a few times until each student has had his or her hands on a few different resources; then the teacher has different students share their information.

- *Treasure Chest:* Use a cardboard box as a treasure chest and fill it with artifacts to create suspense and interest about the topic at hand. The teacher displays a few items and asks the students to predict what the unit will be about. Students can contribute to this treasure chest throughout the unit.

- *Charade the Vocabulary Words:* Students are placed into groups and are given different words to act out from a unit of study. Encourage students to use a dictionary, thesaurus, and other resources to find out the meaning of the words. They act them out and see if their group members can guess the words and what they have in common. Students could also play "against" another group with different words and would then learn twice the number of words.

Making Connections for Learning

After you've grabbed students' attention, it's time to activate their prior knowledge on the topic. Learning is all about connecting the new information with existing understanding. Some ideas to "hook" the new information with existing prior knowledge include:

- Asking what they already know about the topic and share with partners.

◆ Using a premade spinner with questions related to the unit of study, have students spin and share answers within a small group.

◆ Drawing or writing what they know about the concept.

◆ Previewing a book, tagging familiar pictures, and explaining why the pictures were tagged.

Other ways to activate prior knowledge:

◆ *Circle the Sage:* The class is polled to see which students have significant background knowledge on a topic. Those students become the "sages" and they stand in different parts of the room. The teacher divides the remaining students into groups and sends them to different sages. Students rotate until they have heard from each sage.

◆ *Inside/Outside Circles:* The class is divided into two equal groups. One group forms a circle facing outward, the remaining students find one person in the circle to stand opposite, so there are two circles of people facing each other. Questions are posed to get students talking about what they already know about the topic at hand.

◆ *ThinkPad Brainstorming:* Students individually brainstorm and write or draw what they know about a topic. Once they are finished they share their information with a partner or small group. Encourage students to use dry-erase boards, mini chalkboards or gelboards (www.gelboard.com) as their "ThinkPads."

◆ *IIQEE:* This is similar to KWL, but is more fun and allows more students to participate. You can do this whole group, as a small group, or individually. Explain the topic that you are about to teach and ask the students to brainstorm the following statements about the topic (Jensen & Nickelsen, 2008):

I = I think I know….

I = I know that I know….

Q = Questions that I have….

E = Experiences that I've had with this topic….

E = Experiences that my friend(s) have had with this topic….

◆ *Dice-A-Roni:* Provide a die for each group of students (about three students per group). Assign a topic, word, or concept about which questions will be asked. Each number on the die represents a general question that should work for *any* topic you choose. The questions are written on the chalkboard for all to see. Preview each question with the class before they begin. (Jensen & Nickelsen, 2008) For example:

1. What are some facts that you know about this topic?

2. What are some synonyms for this topic? *or* Define this topic in your own words.

3. How could you use this topic currently in your life or in the future? *or* What questions do you have about this topic?

4. Can you think of a specific example of when you experienced this topic? If so, how did it benefit you?

5. If you were writing about this topic, what information would you include?

6. Why might it be important to learn about this topic?

Instruction

The next section of the template is to detail the instruction. The first part of instructional time could be whole group, to teach the "need-to-know" concepts and build common understanding with the class before students begin independent or group-learning tasks. Instruction might include learning activities such as stories, videos, guest speakers, Internet exploration, or other activities that would help students access information. The whole-class-instruction step can be skipped or extended, depending on the needs of the students or your particular objective.

Writing the Objectives

The next step on the template is to create the two or three objectives. Study the pretest results so you know whether two or three tiered objectives should be created. The tiers are:

- *Basic Tier*—For those students who do not yet have the background knowledge to achieve the grade-level standards.

- *Grade-Level Tier*—For those students who have the appropriate background and are ready to work on the grade-level standards.

- *Advanced Tier*—For students who have a depth of background knowledge and whose pretests indicate they have already mastered the standards. They are ready to delve more deeply into the topic.

Write the objective for each tier. The tiering template example (Figure 4.3) contains criteria that every good objective needs. It includes a specific verb and specific content. Within each tier, you will fill in the blanks for that particular group's needs.

Figure 4.3. Tiering Template Example

```
                        EXAMPLE
The students will compare and contrast
                         (Verb)


two branches of government
     (Specific Content)


Assessment: complete an H-diagram or a Venn diagram
```

Explanation of the Tiering Template

♦ *Verb* = Bloom's Taxonomy verb.

Identify a level of thinking as a goal for students in this tier. Processing is thinking; within this section, you are deciding how you want the students to think about the content. We encourage you to choose higher-level verbs as much as possible (see Blackline Master 20 for a list of the Bloom's Taxonomy verbs).

♦ *Specific Content* = Identify the specific content objective.

Using the standards, this is where you write the exact content that you want them to master.

♦ *Assessment* = Commonly understood as the product that shows what the student knows and can do, and its evaluation or judgment against a given benchmark (the standard). This definition actually combines the description of assessment, which often is understood to be the collection of data, including the tools, and evaluation, which is the judgment of that data against a standard.

Learning can be demonstrated in many different ways. Blackline Master 21 contains a list of some of the possibilities. It is also important to identify appropriate assessments for each tier. Students should clearly understand what is expected of them and how they will be evaluated before they begin the task and the assessment should be clearly linked to the standard and objectives.

The Three Tiers

Grade-Level Tier (START HERE)

Many students will be at this "grade-level" tier. This tier starts with the learning standards, the curriculum statement. It is beneficial to begin with this tier because it contains the standard that is required. In fact, if you weren't tiering, this would be the objective you would teach. Choose an activity that has the appropriate concepts and allows for processing the specified objectives.

Basic Tier

Now that the Grade-Level Tier is prepared, it's time to create a Basic Tier task for those students who have not yet acquired the background knowledge or skills to master the objective. What small steps in the skills or content do these students need to support their learning and create a solid basic level of understanding? Figure 4.4 contains examples of how the teacher can structure work for this tier so that it has more support, or scaffolding.

Advanced Tier

Once the Basic and Grade-Level Tiers are prepared, an Advanced Tier task is created for students who show mastery or near mastery of the standard through a preassessment, and now need an opportunity to work in more depth or complexity, or with more open-endedness. Figure 4.4 provides examples of how this might be done with this tier.

To adjust tiers, consider using the strategies outlined in Figure 4.4.

Figure 4.4. Learning Strategies for Tiering

Learning Strategies for the Learner Not Yet at the Standard	Learning Strategies for the Learner Already at the Standard
◆ Provide a graphic organizer—fill parts of it out to get student started.	◆ Have students create their own graphic organizer.
◆ Photocopy sections of text so that students can highlight, place sticky notes in important sections, write their thinking, circle confusing sections, etc.	◆ Provide students with choices on how to process what they are reading (journal entries, split-page processing notes, writing in the margins of photocopied texts, novelty books such as foldable books, etc.).
◆ Provide sentence prompts, question stems, or framed paragraphs to help the student get started.	◆ Use the following dimensions of depth and complexity to add challenge:

- Use as much concrete vocabulary as possible, accompanied by illustrations and symbols (flashcards with pictures; word banks; discussion with words; word walls; lists of questions; lists of signal words).

- Make sure the resources are appropriate.

- Provide a study-buddy or small group support

- Provide more time to complete work.

- Help these students see the pattern behind what they learning (spelling words, roots and affixes, math problems, science, history, etc.).

- Provide templates, sequence of steps, and specific formulas to use.

- Use text-to-speech and/or speech-to-text software.

DEPTH:

1. Give these students more abstract terms related to the concrete terms that they know. Be sure to develop concepts related to the terms.

2. Dive into the specific attributes, traits, and characteristics of the subject matter.

3. Evaluate the factors that influence events (trends).

4. Explore unanswered questions, ambiguities, and gaps of information.

COMPLEXITY:

1. Look at topic from many different perspectives or points of view.

2. Connect the information between, among or within other themes or units of study.

3. Use software programs, such as simulations, to explore concepts more deeply.

4. Change part or all of the content "problem" on which you are working. Exaggerate it or distort it in some way.

Now you have written your tiers within the objective template; you have a strong verb telling you what the students will do with the specific content; and you have written the product or assessment and the criteria that explains their level of accomplishment. Although this planning template outlines three different tiers, you may only require two tiers, or you may need to add additional tiers. The same sequence of steps is followed to add additional tasks.

Groups are then formed based on the preassessments and the specific objective that was written for the small groups. Each group is given specific tasks to complete, based on their readiness. These tasks may include independent or group work and should engage a variety of learning modalities. Additional instructional time may be necessary for the whole group, small groups, or individual students as the work progresses based on formative assessments along the way. You may wish to write names of students on sticky notes (Figure 4.5) and place them on the lesson plan so that you can remove them for the next year if you want to adapt a similar lesson plan. You may also wish to add annotations about how to adjust the lesson if it is done in subsequent years.

Figure 4.5 Student Sticky Note Groups

Group 1(Tier 1) Sean Christine James Noelle	Group 2 (Tier 1) Ashley Lauren Ryan Keaton
Group 3 (Tier 2) Danielle Miller Connor Juan	Group 4 (Tier 3) Kelly Kristen Raul Jamico

Review the Tasks

With the tiering tasks designed, check to make sure that each task is respectful and engaging for each group. Make sure to check that students are in small groups in which they will be successful. The objectives could be written on task cards so that the students know what is expected of them.

Closure

This is how the lesson is wrapped up! An example is to use a Door Pass (Blackline Master 16), which is a summary of their learning. Closure is a very important part of the learning process that improves consolidation of information into memory. Write your closure idea within the appropriate box at the bottom of The Tiered Lesson Plan Template. Some other ideas for closure are:

♦ Define the following words….

- ◆ What would you do if….

- ◆ Explain the _____ process in your own words.

- ◆ Compare and contrast _____ to _____.

For more ideas on closures, see the Self-Reflection sentence starters in Chapter 5 (page 78).

Conduct the Lesson and Assess

Conduct the lesson and evaluate the success of each student. Decide if there are any students who need additional support or challenge. With a colleague, if possible, reflect upon the student learning and how the lesson might be adjusted the next time. The Tiered Lesson Plan Reflection Guide (Blackline Master 19) provides some guiding questions.

Tiered Lesson Plan Examples

Figures 4.6 through 4.14, which appear on page 57 to page 73, are examples of tiered lesson plans. The chapter text continues on page 74.

Figure 4.6. Tiered Lesson Plan: K-2: High-Frequency Words

The Big Picture of the Lesson: **Concept, Skills, Essential Questions, Enduring Understandings or Standard** Recognize high-frequency words.	**Preassessment** Independent reading of a checklist of the first 50 high-frequency words.	**Materials** ♦ Checklist of 50 high-frequency words for teacher ♦ Flashcards of the first 50 words for students ♦ High-Frequency Word Activities for teacher (see Fig. 4.11, page 64)

Grabber & Hook

1. Model lesson: Demonstrate activities using a few of the high frequency word flash cards (e.g., a flashcard game, sorting by beginning sound, making a sentence using the cards). Ask students to think about which one would be the most complex, least complex, and just right activity for them. Discuss how some of these activities would help them learn the word in different ways.
2. Discuss with students: "How many of you would prefer the flashcard game? Sort by beginning sound activity? Make a sentence using the word cards?" Explain that there will be student choice of how to practice the first 10 high-frequency words.

Instruction

1. Prepare activity stations so there are 2 choices at each (e.g., Basic Tier: students write the words on sentence strips and cut out their shape *or* they play the game *Memory* with the 10 words). These stations can be used for each additional set of 10 words that are practiced each week. Remember to have students continually integrate the previously learned words each week in addition to the 10 new words.
2. Students work independently or in small groups at the stations to practice the words in a way that is most beneficial individually.

Basic Tier	Grade Level Tier	Advanced Tier
Possible Choice *This group may need the most teacher help. Students will play a word-matching game that includes reading the words aloud to their small group using the first 10 high-frequency word cards.	*Possible Choice* Students will take turns dictating prewritten sentences with multiple high-frequency words included to their own small group. The students within the group will write a sentence. The reader then can move to the next student.	*Possible Choice* Students will review the high-frequency words along with other words by playing the game *Make It, Mix It, and Fix It* within their small groups. They will write these sentences on a piece of paper to share.

Closure

Ask each student to write on their gelboards (or other student response boards, such as individual white boards), 2 new words that they learned during this exercise (may or may not be the high-frequency words). After giving response time, have the students hold their answer boards up for a quick formative assessment.

Figure 4.7. Tiered Lesson Plan: Character Study—Grades 2–5

The Big Picture of the Lesson: **Concept, Skills, Essential Questions, Enduring Understandings or Standard**	Preassessment	Materials
Identify and describe characters in a story and demonstrate understanding that characters have different qualities that influence their behavior, attitudes and choices.	Ask students to list characteristics of a favorite character from a book. Look to see how specific, accurate, and detailed the list is.	◆ Digital camera ◆ Paper ◆ Story that contains strong character descriptions

Grabber & Hook

Students draw or take digital pictures of themselves. After attaching the photo in the center of a paper, they surround their own picture with words and phrases they would use to describe themselves as a "real-life character." Remind them to use words that describe their physical appearance, emotions, and character traits. We recommend that you create an example about *you*!

Instruction

1. Use the "grabber and hook" activity to discuss the characteristics they used to describe themselves and create categories (e.g., physical characteristics such as tall or short, long or short hair; character traits such as honesty, kindness, or selfish; emotions such as angry, hurt, sad, happy)
2. Discuss how an author's words can help the reader visualize or picture what is really going on in the story, and that characterization is described both explicitly and through inference in words—through descriptive words and expressive actions.
3. Read a story that contains strong character descriptions. Students will choose a character from the story and complete a tiered activity.

Basic Tier	Grade Level Tier	Advanced Tier
Students draw a picture of the story character of choice. They describe the character's traits with words written around the picture and give details of the evidence from the story that supports those characteristics.	Students will create and complete a T-chart to list descriptions of two of the characters from the story and give details of the evidence from the story that supports those characteristics.	Students will use a Venn diagram or H-diagram to compare/contrast two of the story characters and give details of the evidence from the story that supports those characteristics.

Closure

Students share their final products and then reflect, by writing on dry-erase boards, why it is important that we stop while reading to think about character descriptions within the book, whether they are "right there" (explicit descriptions found in the text) or "discovered in their minds using author's clues and their own background knowledge" (implicit).

Figure 4.8. Tiered Lesson Plan: Spelling—Grades 3–5

The Big Picture of the Lesson:	Preassessment	Materials
Concept, Skills, Essential Questions, Enduring Understandings or Standard Spelling patterns can be used to help spell unfamiliar words (e.g., the pattern of ick/ic).	Students are given a diagnostic spelling assessment and placed into flexible groups. These groups will change throughout the year based on ongoing assessments.	♦ 3 leveled spelling lists ♦ Choices for practicing spelling words

Grabber & Hook

1. Students study the following words and see if they can name a rule or pattern that would help them spell the words: trick, brick, music, elastic, hectic, panic, picnic, majestic, quick.
2. Students make the generalization of the spelling pattern "ic/ick" and brainstorm additional words that fit the pattern to the list.

Instruction

Students have their own lists, all with identical spelling patterns, but each list includes words that are at an instructional level for that student.

Basic Tier	Grade Level Tier	Advanced Tier
Students will learn, practice, and be assessed on the following words for this week's spelling lesson of *ick/ic*.	Students will learn, practice, and be assessed on the following words for this week's spelling lesson of *ick/ic*.	Students will learn, practice, and be assessed on the following words for this week's spelling lesson of *ick/ic*.
List 1	**List 2**	**List 3**
sick	tricky	quicksand
trick	sticking	flickering
basic	music	magnetic
public	dramatic	microscopic
metric	traffic	gigantic
mimic	electric	electronic
antics	elastic	arithmetic
frantic	romantic	statistics
plastic	magnetic	majestic
comics	hectic	characteristics

Assign a generic activity that all students will do that works with patterns, structure and meanings. Examples of such activities include:

Patterns	Structure	Meaning
Sort your words into a T-chart based on the spelling patterns ic, ick	Count the number of syllables in each word	Draw a picture that represents the meaning of each word

Figure continues on next page.

Write as many rhyming words as possible that fit with your patterns	Divide each word into syllables	Use your own words to tell about the meaning of each word
Use a highlighter to highlight the patterns in your word	Draw a box around the shape of each word	Write a sentence that shows the meaning of each word
Describe and write the spelling patterns in a way that you could explain to a friend and how you could use it to spell unfamiliar words that fit the same pattern	Make a chart to separate root words and endings	Create a crossword puzzle using your words; include a key

For example, a beginning assignment might be:

1. Sort your words into a T-chart using your spelling patterns
2. Divide your words into syllables
3. Draw a picture that represents the meaning of your words.

Generic activities may also be placed at a learning station, and the teacher can select activities that are "must dos" and those that they may choose from ("may dos").

Practice

Students choose from a number of ways to practice their spelling words, such as:

Look/say/write your words using:
- Individual gel boards
- Individual white boards
- Wikki Stix
- Salt boxes
- Gelatin powder
- Sandpaper
- Shaving cream
- Pudding
- Carpet
- Plastic letters or letter tiles

Closure

Ask students to evaluate whether the words on their lists were a good fit, a nice challenge, or too difficult. Ask them to explain how they did on their practice assignments, and how the new spelling rule can help them to figure out the spelling of other ick/ic words.

Three levels of spelling lists isn't a requirement. You can increase or decrease the number of lists used, depending on the readiness levels of learners in your classroom. Figure 4.9 is an example from a tiered spelling program.

Figure 4.9. Tiered Lesson Plan: Vocabulary Processing—Grades 6–8

The Big Picture of the Lesson: Concept, Skills, Essential Questions, Enduring Understandings or Standard	Preassessment	Materials
Reviewing and elaborating on content-area vocabulary words from the American Revolution unit.	Cloze assessment in which students choose the appropriate vocabulary word to place within a paragraph about the American Revolution.	♦ List A, List B, List C ♦ Topic-specific cloze preassessment ♦ Vocabulary list

Grabber & Hook

Ask students to turn to a partner and choose 3 of the vocabulary words within a topic of study that seem to be the most difficult to recall or define. Write these words on a sticky note and compare the list to their partner's list to see which ones are similar. Tell the students that they are going to do something special with these 3 words so that they can remember them for a lifetime!

Instruction

1. Students are placed into small groups depending on the preassessment results.
2. Students each receive 3 blank sheets of paper. Ask them to fold the sheets of paper so that there are 6 boxes total on one page. These are called *2-4-6-8 boxes*.
3. With the paper landscape-oriented and flat on a desk, have the students write 1 vocabulary word in color on each page on the center middle line.
4. Students choose several ways to process their vocabulary words from their specified list (see List A, List B, or List C). Each processing choice is expressed within one of the boxes created by folding the paper. In other words, students will process each of their 3 vocabulary words 6 different ways.

Figure continues on next page.

Basic Tier	Grade Level Tier	Advanced Tier
Students will process their vocabulary words in the following ways:	Students will process their vocabulary words in the following ways:	Students will process their vocabulary words in the following ways:
LIST A	**LIST B**	**LIST C**
Define the vocabulary term in your own words Write a meaningful sentence List characteristics of the word Create a rhyme, pun, or cartoon List synonyms List antonyms List other meanings for the word List words with the same spelling pattern Draw a picture to help you remember the word	Explain how and when you would use the word List 3 examples of the word Use a web to connect the word to 4 related words or concepts List 2 ways you might use the word in the future Use the word in a question or exclamatory sentence Divide the word into syllables; mark the stressed syllable Add a prefix or suffix; explain how the word's meaning changes. Create a simile or metaphor Use the word in an analogy Summarize what you know about the word in a sentence	What are your opinions and feelings about the word? Connect the word to your life How does the word relate to current world events? Create a "what if" question with the word List the pros and cons of the word With 3 as high importance, rate the word 1, 2, or 3 based on how important you think it is for this unit Create an acronym to explain what it means Research the etymology (history) of the word

Closure

To help all students review all of the words, collect the completed 2-4-6-8 boxes, sort them according to the word, and then have students teach the words to the whole class (so that each word is taught once).

Figure 4.10. Tiered Lesson Plan: Word Choice in Writing—2–3-Day Lesson Plan—Grades 6–8

The Big Picture of the Lesson: **Concept, Skills, Essential Questions, Enduring Understandings or Standard** Word choice can add interest and strength to a piece of writing.	**Preassessment** Use a previously written assignment where the teacher or student determines that word choice could be stronger. Use preassessment to divide students into groups.	**Materials** ◆ Paper and pencil for each student ◆ Rate Your Wording Rubric—General List (Figures 4.13, page 68, and 4.14, page 69)

Grabber & Hook

1. As a class, examine a favorite book that has strong word choice (e.g., *Maniac Magee* by Jerry Spinelli). Show the "Rate Your Wording Rubric—General List" and discuss the strength of word choice from the book. Notice there are many aspects to good word choice in writing.
2. Have them assess the book with the "Rate Their Wording Rubric—General List" by listing specific examples of "Dull, Decent, or Dynamic" word choices.

Instructions

1. Once students are in their groups, instruct each group on the word choice focus for the next piece of writing. For example, List A students might have a mini-lesson on using strong adverbs or adjectives.
2. Model and "think aloud" while students watch and help make revisions to a piece of writing.
3. Students then make revisions to their work, based on the mini-lesson and the lesson modeled.
4. Make sure that you explicitly teach each component of good word choice that is listed on their specific rubric.

Basic Tier	**Grade Level Tier**	**Advanced Tier**
Students edit a piece of writing and focus their word choice elaboration options on the following: List A Examples ◆ Synonyms ◆ Adjectives ◆ Adverbs ◆ Description ◆ Detail ◆ Rubric: Have students create specific criteria for their list (see example)	Students edit a piece of writing and focus their word choice elaboration options on the following: List B Examples ◆ Similes ◆ Superlatives ◆ Comparisons ◆ Rubric: Have students create specific criteria for their list (see example)	Students edit a piece of writing and focus their word choice elaboration options on the following: List C Examples ◆ Dialogue ◆ Metaphors ◆ Analogies ◆ Personification ◆ Rubric: Have students create specific criteria for their list (see example)

Closure

Students exchange their writing and provide feedback on the edited writing using the "Rate Their Writing" rubric. They should discuss how the revisions make the piece of writing stronger and if there are any other suggestions based on the rubric that might be helpful. Provide positive verbal feedback and acknowledge the way the students elaborated within their writing.

Figure 4.11. High-Frequency Word Activities

These activities can be used within centers or can be sent home as "practices." Choose the appropriate activity level based on the readiness of each student.

Basic Tier

♦ Read the words aloud together; choral read the spelling.

♦ Chant the words with funny voices over and over, or shout it out loud like a cheerleader.

♦ Cut out the words to see the shape.

♦ Write the words in the air. Erase. Write them again.

♦ Write the words on paper and say the letter name out loud as you write.

♦ Make the words using magnetic letters on a cookie sheet, or build words with word tiles.

♦ Play the game *Memory* with the words.

♦ Use words to play *Bingo*.

♦ Use play-dough or *Wikki Stix* to make the words.

♦ Write the words in shaving cream on a tray, or in gelatin powder in a pan or on a sheet of wax paper.

Grade-Level Tier

♦ Dictate a sentence with a high-frequency word included in the sentence.

♦ Sort the words by beginning, middle, and ending sounds.

♦ Locate the words in books that you are reading.

♦ Use a highlighter to hunt for the words in newspapers, magazines, on cereal boxes, etc.

♦ File the words in alphabetical order within a word file box.

♦ Use 5 or fewer of the high-frequency words to tell or write a story (semantic story design).

Advanced Tier

♦ Sort, classify, and label the words in at least 2 ways.

♦ Make a sentence using the word cards. (Use extra cards to write the words needed to complete the sentence.)

♦ Make It, Mix It, and Fix It—Build a sentence, mix the words up, and then put the word cards in order again. Have a friend try to put the words in order to make your sentence.

♦ Use the ABC Card File Box as a dictionary when writing.

♦ Make a crossword puzzle for others to try.

Figure 4.12. Rate Your Wording Rubrics in 3 Parts

Rate Your Wording Rubric (1 of 3)

Name: _____

List A

Instructions: Check to indicate your rating of the word choice, based on the identified criteria. Then write two positive pieces of feedback ("Two to Glow") and one thing to work on ("One to Grow").

Criteria	1–Dull	2–Decent	3–Dynamic
1. Synonyms			
2. Adjectives			
3. Adverbs			
4. Description			
5. Detail			
6. Mechanics (spelling, grammar, punctuation, etc.)			
7. Other:			
TOTAL:			

Two to Glow:

One to Grow:

Name: _____

List B

Instructions: Check to indicate your rating of the word choice, based on the identified criteria. Then write two positive pieces of feedback ("Two to Glow") and one thing to work on ("One to Grow").

Criteria	1–Dull	2–Decent	3–Dynamic
1. Similes			
2. Superlatives			
3. Comparatives			
4. Mechanics (spelling, grammar, punctuation, etc.)			
5. Other:			
Total:			

Two to Glow:

One to Grow:

Figure continues on next page.

Name: _____

List C

Instructions: Check to indicate your rating of the word choice, based on the identified criteria. Then write two positive pieces of feedback ("Two to Glow") and one thing to work on ("One to Grow").

Criteria	1–Dull	2–Decent	3–Dynamic
1. Dialogue			
2. Metaphors			
3. Analogies			
4. Personifications			
5. Mechanics (spelling, grammar, punctuation, etc.)			
6. Other:			
TOTAL:			

Two to Glow:

One to Grow:

Figure 4.13. Rate Your Wording Rubric—General List

Name: _____

Title of Writing: _____

DYNAMIC Word Choice Characteristics

Words convey the intended message in an accurate, interesting, and unique way.
- Specific and accurate words
- Meaning of writing is clear
- Contains lively verbs, colorful adjectives, precise adverbs
- Natural word choice
- Memorable and striking phrases and words
- Effective dialogue
- Figures of speech used powerfully

DECENT Word Choice Characteristics

The language has meaning and is clear, but it is not striking
- Writing doesn't quite hold audience's attention
- Some evidence of descriptive, colorful and lively words
- Wording is a bit awkward rather than a natural speech pattern
- Writer keeps word choice at a very safe level rather than taking a risk with new and unique words
- Few figures of speech (or used inaccurately)
- Little dialogue or dialogue that does not enhance the writing
- Some effort made to use better word choice

DULL Word Choice Characteristics

Vocabulary is limited, meaning of writing is unclear, and little effort was made to improve word choice.
- Language is vague and redundant
- Meaning is unclear
- Words are used incorrectly
- Weak word choice
- Figures of speech not used

Figure 4.14. More Tiered Lesson Ideas: Examples for Younger Students

These "starters" may provide ideas to use as a springboard for more detailed lessons, that you can tailor for the needs of your students. There are a variety of subjects and grade levels represented; some have ideas for two tiers and others for three.

Math—Sorting

Basic: Sort objects that differ by only 2 characteristics with the support of graphic organizers (e.g., color, shape, into 2 or more different groups (big/small; red/blue/green) and explain how they are grouped.

Standard: Sort objects that differ by 3 characteristics. Students should identify each group; and then regroup the same objects into a second different set of categories.

Advanced: Students create a Venn or H diagram, and sort objects provided on the organizer. They should state how the properties of the items cause them to fit into the specific sections of the organizers.

Reading—Comprehension Through Retelling

Basic: Students will use 4–6 pictures representing the text from a story. Students sequence pictures and retell the story.

Standard: Students will be able to read a story and retell the story with as many details as possible.

Science—Describing Objects by Their Properties

Standard: Students are given a variety of objects inside numbered plastic sandwich bags. Along with the items are slips of tag board that have words describing each object. The students match the cards to the items, and then self-check their work by turning over the cards and matching its number with the sandwich bag number.

Advanced: Students find their own objects/materials and create their own word-description cards with the answers on the back. These tasks can be shared with other students.

Social Studies: Understanding Change Over Time

Basic: Students create a timeline with their own baby pictures (or pictures of a child growing from an infant to an older child) and describe and give examples of how they have changed over time.

Figure continues on next page.

Standard: Students choose from various sets of cards that show change over time to place in sequence from earlier time to the present. These cards might represent transportation (automobiles, planes, or trains), clothing styles, or communication (letters, telegraph, computer, etc.). They describe and give examples of how these things have shown change over time and what some of the factors might have been to influence the change.

Computers: Using Drawing Programs to Represent the Main Idea

Basic: Students use a drawing program to create a slide or slides that summarize the main idea of a story, video, field trip, guest speaker, etc. They should be able to tell why their picture(s) represents the main idea.

Standard: Students use a drawing program to create a slide or slides about the main idea and link them together in a slide show. They should be able to describe in detail why their pictures represent the main idea.

Advanced: Students use a drawing program to create a slide about the main idea and then create an additional slide or slides that compares the main idea to another story, event, etc.

Math—Using Mean, Median and Mode

All: Hold a "Student Olympics" where students participate in different events and collect data from each event.

Standard: Students use the data collected from the "Student Olympics" to find each of the three measures of central tendency (mean, median, and mode) using supportive tools such as websites, calculators, and step-by-step instructions.

Advanced: Students use the information collected (mean, median, mode) from the activities to write and answer questions about the set of data.

Writing—Friendly Letter

Basic: Give students a template of a friendly letter with some parts complete and some blanks. Students complete the friendly letter by filling in the pieces of the template.

Standard: Give students a graphic organizer that shows the parts of a friendly letter. Using the organizer, have them write a friendly letter to someone they know.

Advanced: Students write a friendly letter independently.

English—Summarizing Fiction

Basic: Students summarize a book or chapter by writing within a web, including who did what, where, when, why and how.

Standard: Students summarize a book or chapter by completing the following template within 1 paragraph: Somebody wanted to _____, but _____, so _____ and _____.

Advanced: Students summarize a book or chapter by being as concise as possible. They need to pretend that they are paying $1.00 for each word used and yet be able to explain the gist of the book so that a person reading their summarization can decide whether or not they want to read the book. The goal is to write the summary in as few words as possible.

Science—Erosion

Basic: Using a sequence of pictures describe the process of erosion.

Standard: Describe the process of erosion using found objects or pictures, or use a digital camera to photograph and describe examples of erosion around the school property.

Advanced: Think of an unlikely comparison for the process of erosion and describe how they could be related and why.

Internet Research

Basic: Use the site specified by the teacher and a text-to-speech reader (e.g., www.naturalreaders.com). Summarize the information orally.

Standard: Use the site specified by the teacher. Read and summarize the information using a graphic organizer.

Advanced: Find a site that describes ideas similar to the one chosen by the teacher. Read and summarize the information and describe the similarities using a graphic organizer as a guide.

Physical Education—Passing a Soccer Ball

Basic: In partners, pass a soccer ball back and forth. Practice closer together and farther apart.

Standard: Pass a soccer ball back and forth with a partner while navigating a simple course marked by pylons.

Figure continues on next page.

Advanced: Work with a partner and choose to be the offensive or defensive team. Find another two-person team to challenge your team. Work through a complex pylon course while passing the soccer ball between partners and trying to take or keep the ball away from the other team. Switch roles.

English—Vocabulary: List-Sort-Label

Basic: Students use words from a unit of study and write each on a 3×5 card. Then they sort them into categories provided by the teacher.

Standard: Students write each of the words from a unit of study on a 3×5 card. Next, they sort them into similar groups. Using sticky notes, they label them with a word that describes the category.

Advanced: Students brainstorm words from a unit of study and write each on a 3×5 card. Next, they sort them into similar groups and using sticky notes, label them with a word that describes the category. Finally, the students see if they can rearrange the cards to create different categories.

Foreign Language—Developing Vocabulary in a Second Language

Basic: In partners, students walk around the room touching various objects with a pointer and take turns reading the names of the objects from the attached cards. The words are listed first in English and then in the second language.

Standard: Students walk around the school and create/post labels for objects they see in both English and a second language

Advanced: Using words found in the classroom, construct a dialogue in a second language that uses as many of the words as possible.

Math—Using Percentages to Solve Real-World Problems

Basic: Using a supportive graphic organizer, students calculate sales tax on items they would like to purchase from newspaper flyers and calculate the total that would be owed if the items were purchased.

Standard: Students calculate sales tax on items they would like to purchase from newspaper flyers and calculate the total amount that would be owed if the items were purchased.

Social Studies—Understanding Key Historical Figures

Basic: Using selected documented sources and a graphic organizer that is provided by the teacher, describe the contributions and roles of a person who had an impact on history.

Standard: Using at least two documented resources of your choosing, and a graphic organizer of your choice, describe the contributions and roles of a person who had an impact on history.

Advanced: Using three or more documented resources, create a product or presentation that describes the contributions and roles of a person who had an impact on history.

Science—Designing Scientific Investigations

Basic: Using a graphic organizer and step-by-step instructions, design an investigation to test individual variables using scientific processes.

Standard: Design an investigation to test individual variables using scientific processes.

Advanced: Design an investigation to test multiple variables using scientific processes.

Health—Understanding How Nutrients are Used by the Human Body

Basic: From a set of index cards provided by the teacher that list nutrients and classifications, sort the cards and then describe how those nutrients are used in the body.

Standard: From a set of index cards provided by the teacher, create your own classification for nutrients and describe how they are used in the body.

Advanced: Compare nutrients to real world or story characters to tell about how they are classified and how they are used in the body.

Tying Things Together

This chapter provides a lesson-planning template and step-by-step instructions for creating a tiered lesson. It also outlines ways to add or remove elements such as supports, depth and complexity, and has a wide range of sample lessons. Chapter 5 discusses assessment and tiering.

For Further Reflection

♦ How might I use the Tiered Lesson Plan Template to help adjust instruction to meet the needs of learners?

♦ How else can I adjust elements such as supports, depth, and complexity of tasks?

♦ How can I use the lesson examples as ideas for planning for the needs of my students?

5

Passing Final Inspection: Assessment of Tiered Products

The educator must believe in the potential power of his pupil, and he must employ all his art in seeking to bring his pupil to experience this power.

—Alfred Adler

As the end of the "project" draws near, the architect, the contractor, all the managers, and the client anxiously await the final scrutiny by state and local inspectors to see if all the sections of the building meet or exceed code, and the plans come together to create a great impact on the architectural community. It is more likely that this will be a positive experience when the benchmarks are set up at the onset of the project and are checked, reinstructed, and retested along the way, with everyone knowing the direction and the timetable of the project from start to finish. The same is true for effective instruction.

How to Assess Tiered Assignments

There are many different opportunities to assess students during tiered instruction.

Summative Assessment

Summative assessments reflect most, if not all, of the essential knowledge that is required by the state/provincial standards. Although many teachers believe that a summative assessment is one big comprehensive assessment at the end of a unit of study that attempts to test as much of the skills and knowledge as possible, a summative assessment can instead include a variety of opportunities, like focused short quizzes at the end of a chunk of learning; projects; presentations; demonstrations; written assignments; efficient, focused end-of-the-unit tests; and self-evaluations. As a unit of study begins, the students are made aware of the standards to be met and what it looks like to meet those expectations within the assessments. Will there be projects and presentations? Will there be graded quizzes after small chunks of learning? Summative assessments are given when students have been given multiple opportunities to process the information, have been given feedback, and are ready to show what they know and can do.

Formative Assessment

Formative assessment of student learning is integrated into teaching and learning. During a unit of study, assignments to process new material are given to students so that they have an opportunity to make sense and meaning of new information and skills. Guidelines for assessing this work is essential, not for grading purposes as the students are still practicing, but because the students need to have a guideline for recognizing mastery or for understanding their proficiency. These guidelines can include scoring guides or rubrics, checklists for the students and teachers, scope and sequence charts, benchmark papers, and the exit standards. This type of assessment enables the teacher to make decisions about the direction of the day's instruction or individual instruction for specific students.

Some tiered processing assignments require little more than self-checking opportunities and a way to self-regulate the completion of activities assigned. All children need to be responsible for their own behavior and academics within the work station time in which they are completing tiered assignments. During this period the teacher may be fielding questions and giving feedback to various students within the classroom as independent and small group work progresses.

Self-Checking

Making activities as self-checking as possible is efficient for the teacher and provides immediate feedback to the students. For example, in the lesson plan "Reading—Comprehension Through Use of Retelling," self-checking consists of ordering pictures in a sequence and checking the numbers written on the back to ensure the retelling process was placed in sequential order. The students check to see if their first prediction is correct by turning over the cards and checking the sequential numbers on the backs of the cards. For self-checking examples with other content, students can look at the complete poem from the text to see if they placed the strips in the correct order. In the foreign language class, the English word can be on one side of the card, and the second language word on the opposite side, so a student can read either alone or with a partner.

Self-Reflections

Often, students and teachers alike find value only in the feedback that is given by peers, teachers, and administrators. It is just as valuable to stop and reflect on our own learning. Self-reflection gives us the time to "check our work over and make changes to benefit it, to ask deeper questions of our own work, to try something new, creative, and different with the work we are doing, and to find wonder and awe in the new learning around us." According to Arthur L. Costa and Bena Kallick in *Habits of Mind* (2000), these are dispositions displayed by intelligent people as they respond to life and learning. This type of self-reflection should not happen only at the end of a unit of study. It is part of the learning itself. Just as we teach the multiplication tables, the sounds of the letters, and how to analyze a poem, we should also teach students how to self-reflect as part of assessing their own understanding. Blackline Masters 12 and 13 are reflection tools suitable for both younger and older students.

As a new task is being processed, a student could stop during the work and ask a series of questions. Some of the questions below are better suited to some tasks such as reading for information, others are more suited for writing tasks, and others are more suited for assignments that result in projects. Responding to questions should be modeled with the class so that students can get a good feel for the deep level of thinking that is involved in metacognition.

Some questions or prompts that can be used in self-reflections are the following:

- ♦ I can see a pattern in my work....
- ♦ This is similar to....
- ♦ I noticed that....
- ♦ Can I identify the parts of this problem?
- ♦ I liked....
- ♦ This work reminds me of....
- ♦ The part of the work that frustrated me was....
- ♦ Before I did this...I thought..., but now I think....

- I am still confused by....
- In correcting my work I found my mistake, and....
- My next steps would be....
- What other way could I have planned this?
- The main idea in my work is....
- The author is trying to tell me that....
- I'd like to learn more about....
- I predict....
- I wonder....
- My answer is different than the answer of others because....
- My answer does (does not) make sense because....
- When you explained it, I began to think that....
- What ideas justify my answer?
- What inference could I make about this work?
- How could I apply what I've learned to something I know about the world?
- What new questions does this bring to my mind?
- What conclusions can I draw?
- Could I classify this new knowledge in some way?
- How would I rephrase this information to make sense of it?

Students can choose one of these questions or be assigned one of them.

More Self-Reflection Ideas

"Dear Teacher" Notes

Students use index cards to write "notes" to the teacher that describe what they are learning in a particular unit of study (Blackline Master 22). They can describe what they see as their strengths and/or they can request additional help with particular skills or information. The teacher can answer the student directly during small group time or can answer the question in a general way to the whole class if the letter is anonymous.

Two-Minute Quick Writes

Students respond to a prompt or a question, or to an experience in a journal or a notebook.

Reflecting on the "Construction" of My Learning

Students reflect on their own completed project and describe two things they did well and one part of the project that they would do differently on a similar project in the future. This tool could also be used as a framework for peer feedback.

Figure 5.1. Reflecting on the "Construction" of My Learning

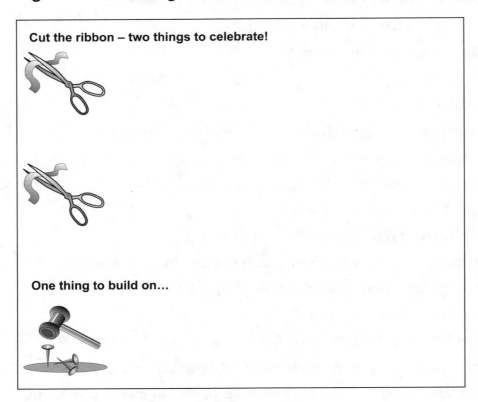

Cut the ribbon – two things to celebrate!

One thing to build on...

Personal Reflection on Processing

Ask students to reflect personally on how they processed what they have learned. They can think about background knowledge before the learning and after the learning; list the ways that they processed the content and how they deepened their understanding of the concept, what the most valuable learning was, and create a "next step" plan. Blackline Master 23 could be used to guide their personal reflection on the processing for the assignment. (Jensen & Nickelsen, 2008)

Checklists

Checklists can be used to create a series of tasks students complete. The checklists are not used to judge the level of quality of the work, but a "sense of what should be included and what is expected. Rubrics could later be turned into checklists, where each item on the checklist could have a corresponding description of the quality of work expected.

An example of using a checklist in this way would be to have students read a short story, passages, or picture book, then choose one of the prompts from the list below. The prompts could be revised based on the selection the teacher assigns. The prompts can also be tiered. In this example, the first item is easier to respond to than the next, the second is easier than the third, etc.

- ◆ Draw a "moment-in-time" from the story.

    Checklist:

    ☐ Sketch shows a snapshot view of action within the story or passage.

    ☐ Audience can read the scene from the sketch.

- ◆ Create a timeline that shows the events in the main character's life in the period with the story.

    Checklist:

    ☐ Timeline is created in sensible chunks within the life-period of the story.

    ☐ Important events of the story are evidenced.

    ☐ Important events of the character's life are connected to either the student's life, another character from another story, or the world at large.

- ◆ Rewrite the ending of the story.

    Checklist:

    ☐ Story ending is connected sensibly to the beginning and middle of the story.

    ☐ The main character is evidenced in the end of the story.

    ☐ The ending elicits excitement, sadness, surprise, amazement, or other emotions.

Cubing

Cubing is another tiered assignment possibility for the classroom. Cubing can be used as a strategy for processing new content, and it can also be used as a formative assessment. When the unit is coming to a conclusion, teachers can use this strategy with small groups of students who are working at the same levels. The leveled questions can be placed on a cube itself, or the questions can be on a leveled task card and a numbered cube is rolled and matched then with the related questions on the task card. As students in the small groups take turns rolling the cube and answering the questions asked on the task cards, the teacher takes anecdotal notes and makes decisions on any reteaching that may be necessary before a graded quiz. When students have completed their individual tasks, the students can share their work with the small group and then the whole group.

Rubrics and Scoring Guides

Quite simply, rubrics, or scoring guides, are tools for teachers and students that define what is expected of the student to meet a certain level of proficiency. They are sets of standards and criteria that are linked to learning objectives. Rubrics help students and teachers understand the quality of work expected and by having students participate in creating the criteria, they have more ownership in the end products and presentations. They have a target. They know when their work is incomplete and what they must do to finish it accurately and well. Rubrics make it easier for the teacher to assess assignments as the criteria are well explained, and they make expectations clearer to parents. Rubrics and scoring guides can also be used for self-evaluation, reflection, and peer and parent review.

Some rubrics are holistic in nature and consider all criteria of the same importance, whereas an analytic rubric breaks the tasks and concepts down into smaller pieces so that they can be assessed in each area. Descriptors may also be weighted based on the importance of the concept taught at that time.

Rubrics should address:

♦ What the essential and enduring content and skills are to be addressed.

♦ What the key learning looks like.

♦ Standards specified performance levels (what you must demonstrate to be assessed at a certain level).

Bullets could be highlighted within the columns that best fit the work showcased by the student. Sometimes the content, product, and presentation may have highlights in several columns, but would be substantially stronger in one area as opposed to another.

Interviews and Conferences as Assessment Tools

Interviews and conferences with students can be used to show growth over time. These discussions are based on the standards that the individual student is expected to meet during the course of the grading period. The students can also discuss their own learning and can evaluate their own progress against the standards. In *Transforming Classroom Grading* (2000), Robert Marzano says the true spirit of effective assessment is when the teacher and student collaborate as they analyze the student's strengths and weaknesses based on the standards.

What About Grading?

When the assignments and assessments are completed, and when the rubrics and checklists have guided the learning, one onerous question remains: How do I grade a tiered task? Do I grade students strictly against the standards or against the students themselves and their own improvement? Is there room for a bit of both? Whichever we choose we must do it with the understanding that it should help students move forward toward mastery of the standards and confidence in their abilities as a learner.

Figure 5.2. Tiered Assignment Rubric Sample

Criteria	Emergent	Developing	Knowledgeable	Outstanding
Content	• Some inaccurate content • Content addressed may not quite answer the question • Content does not demonstrate understanding	• Mostly accurate content • Content addresses most of the question • Content demonstrates some understanding	• Accurate content • Content addresses the question • Content contains demonstrates understanding	• Content is accurate, clear, and detailed • Content goes beyond addressing the question • Content demonstrates deep understanding
Resulting Product	• Product was completed quickly and with little planning • Product gives little information to the audience	• Product is generally well-planned • Product gives some information to the audience	• Product is well-planned and organized • Product informs the audience	• Product is exceptionally well-planned, organized and executed • Product informs and interests the audience
Presentation	• Question/objective of assignment was not shared with the audience • Presentation shows little evidence of planning and practice	• Question/objective of project was unclear to the audience • Presentation shows some evidence of planning and practice	• Question/objective was shared with the audience • Presentation is organized, planned, and practiced	• Question/objective was stated and reason for choice is given • Presentation is well-planned organized and practiced
Resources	• No resources used	• Used some resources	• Used many resources	• Used many resources of a wide variety

A rubric that describes the quality of the product has in itself documented the level of mastery through its descriptions. That's assessment. However, some schools or districts require that a second source of reporting be included (e.g., letter grades, anecdotal notes, 1 to 5 number scale, percentage scores). That's grading. Tiered lessons that are designed to help students process new content are not graded. Tiered homework assignments that are given after students have mastered the content, but are still practicing, rehearsing, and reviewing are not graded. In *Transformative Assessment* (2008), W. James Popham explains that the function of formative assessment's evidence gathering is to enhance students' learning, not to compare students' performances with one another.

He goes on to say that "none of the assessments functioning as part of the formative assessment process ought to be graded" (pages 88–89). When students have learned the content, have practiced, have had feedback, and have practiced some more, then they are ready to be assigned tasks and summative assessments for grading.

Districts, schools, and individual teachers have different definitions of what letter grades indicate. For example, if a student follows your expectations for meeting proficiency in a content area at a specific grade level on a particular standard, does that student receive an A grade for completing everything you asked, or a B grade for meeting the high standard benchmark your school has set? And is there a C grade for meeting the standard at a very baseline level? Have you shared the expectations for how they can reach an A?

Some teachers believe that if students just meet the expectations that are set, then the students have earned an A. With this in mind, the grading scale is the same for all standards-based assessments at all tiers. But what if we adjust the curriculum for the gifted student or restructure it for students who are struggling with the curriculum the way it stands for proficiency? Is it possible to structure support and differentiation so that struggling students can get close to proficiency with an honestly earned grade of C, and all the learning community, including the families, can celebrate the true merit of that grade? Rick Wormeli recommends erring on the side of hope. In *Fair Isn't Always Equal* (2006), he explains that when a student makes a significant amount of growth during a grading period but still has not mastered the standards set for proficiency, that we might consider "recording the grade that represents the student's accomplishments and learning" (page 175). In the end, there is no easy answer to this question, but how grading is conducted and reported are largely determined by district and school policy, to which we must adhere.

Tying Things Together

This chapter provides information on how to incorporate assessment within tiered assignments and tiered assessments. It provides some helpful hints about using checklists, rubrics, and grades for tiered work, and has examples of self-assessments and strategies for assessments.

For Further Reflection

- How do I choose the best assessment formats for my tiered assignments?
- How do I decide what "meeting the standard" actually looks like?
- How do I use a variety of assessments over the course of a unit of study?

6

Cutting the Tape: Time to Start Tiering!

At the end of a construction project, the designers and workers gather together to celebrate what they have built. They reflect on the project and cut the ribbon to officially open the structure. Just as constructing a building is a process that involves planning and dedication, so is the process of learning to tier instruction.

Don't try to tier everything tomorrow! Instead, take baby steps toward the big goal of tiering. Make sure you feel comfortable with the following tasks before creating that tiered lesson plan.

- Students are working in cooperative groups well. There are rules, role cards, high expectations, and routines in place during grouping time that keep the students on task.

- You feel comfortable writing daily differentiated lesson plan with a strong objective.

- You feel comfortable with preassessing your students and evaluating the data so that changes are made to improve your instruction.

- You know your students well—how they learn, process, and work with other students.

- You have several ideas on how to differentiate one objective.

We also want to remind you that our first attempts at tiered lessons were far from perfect, but we learned so much from those experiences. We believe that mistakes are wonderful ways to learn how to do something correctly! Each tiered lesson that we created only got better and easier to create.

Parting Words

Teaching is one of those rare professions where what you do can impact the life of a child forever. It may not be something that is reflected upon frequently, but its truth is evident every time someone tells a story about how a teacher positively affected their lives. Is the effort put into tiering instruction worth it? Absolutely! If instruction can be matched to students' "just right" level, they will continue to learn and grow.

Even though the research on the science of teaching is constantly growing, it is still not exact, nor will it ever be. We must be willing to continue to try new things, and to constantly work to do what is right for our students.

> *What is important is to keep learning, to enjoy the challenge and to tolerate ambiguity. In the end, there are no certain answers.*

—Martina Homer

Appendix

Blackline Masters

Name _____

Uniqueness Bingo!

Instructions: Circulate around the room and have classmates sign one square with their name and one unique thing about themselves.

Blackline Master 2a

My Learning Strengths at School

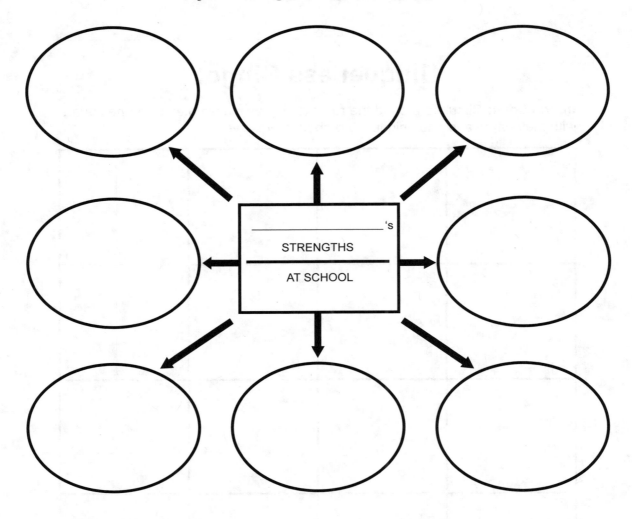

Blackline Master 2b

My Learning Strengths at Home

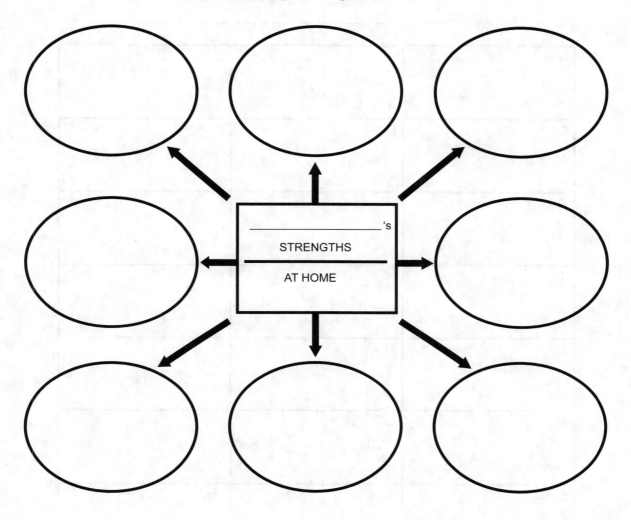

Inside the center box:

_____'s

STRENGTHS

AT HOME

Blackline Master 3
ABC Brainstorm

Topic: _____

A	B	C
D	E	F
G	H	I
J	K	L
M	N	O
P	Q	R
S	T	U
V	W	XYZ

Blackline Master 4
Task Assignment Details

Group Name: _____

Names of Students in Group:

_____

_____

_____

Assignment Directions:

1.

2.

3.

4.

5.

6.

Blackline Master 5

Learning Station Work Schedule

Work Choices
Must Do:
1.
2.
3.
4.
5.
May Do:
6.
7.
8.

Blackline Master 6
Group Work Expectation Poster

Date: _____

Activity Title: _____

1. Our Group Rules are:
2. The Roles Cards that we will be using today are:
3. The Learning Goal:

4. General Directions:
    ♦ Time allotted: _____
    ♦ Turn in work in the following place: _____
    ♦ Do the following when finished: _____

5. Reminders:

Blackline Master 7

Group Task Cards for Younger Students (1 of 2)

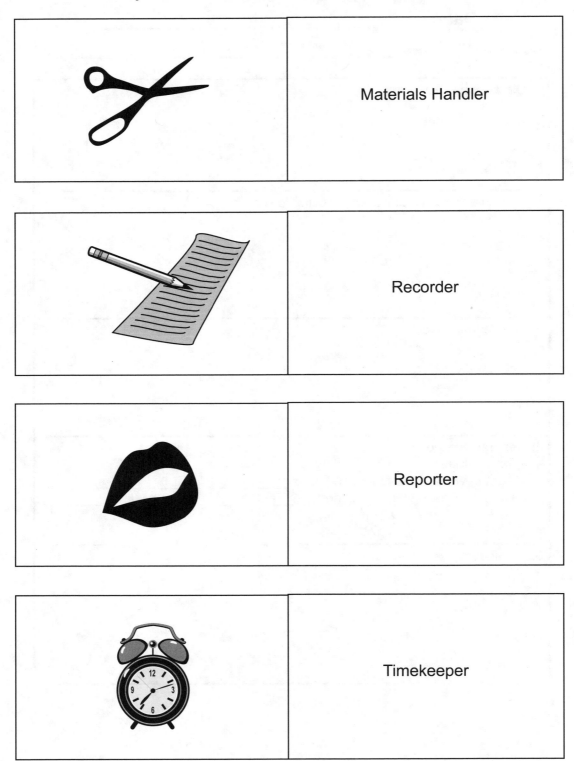

	Materials Handler
	Recorder
	Reporter
	Timekeeper

Task Master

Hitchhiker

Encouragers

	Materials Handler	Gather materials to do the task, hold chart paper or other material for reporter, post or place group work on display.
	Recorder	Write down or draw group ideas.
	Reporter	Share group ideas with the class.
	Timekeeper	Note the start time and end time for the activity. Give the groups prompts at 5 minute intervals.

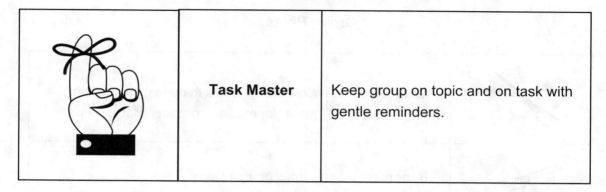	**Task Master**	Keep group on topic and on task with gentle reminders.
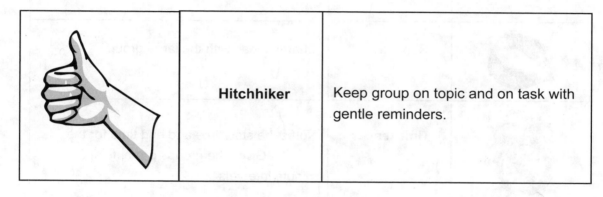	**Hitchhiker**	Keep group on topic and on task with gentle reminders.
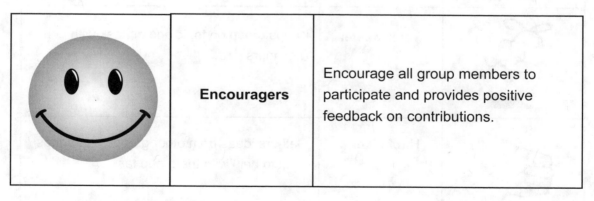	**Encouragers**	Encourage all group members to participate and provides positive feedback on contributions.

Blackline Master 9

Learning Contract—Group Work (1 of 2)

Group Roles

	Materials	Collects materials to do task, holds chart paper for reporter, posts products on walls
	Recorder	Writes group ideas
	Reporter	Shares ideas with the large group
	Timekeeper	Notes the start time and end time for the activity. Gives the groups prompts at 5 minute intervals
	Task Master	Keeps group on topic and on task with gentle reminders
	Hitchhiker	Gathers ideas from other groups and brings back to help with the group task
	Encouragers	Encourages all group members to participate and provides positive feedback on contributions

Learning Contract—Group Work (2 of 2)

Group Members: _____

Group Task: _____

Group Responsibilities: _____

_____

Our project will be complete by: _____

Group Roles:

Materials will be handled by: _____

Recording will be done by: _____

Reporting to the class will be done by: _____

Time for our task will be kept by: _____

The task master for our project will be: _____

The encourager(s) for our project will be: _____

We agree that we will perform our individual duties and work as a whole to the best of our ability and commit to keep the group working together well. If we have problems, we agree to try to resolve them together first and then ask for help if necessary.

Student Signatures:

Teacher Signature: _____

Blackline Master 10
"Please Help" Tent Cards

Instructions: Copy this on heavyweight paper or tagboard for added strength. Fold on dotted line. Students place the "please help" sign on their table/desks if they need help, and face down if they are working independently. (Only one card per table or group is needed.)

TAB FOR GLUE/TAPE

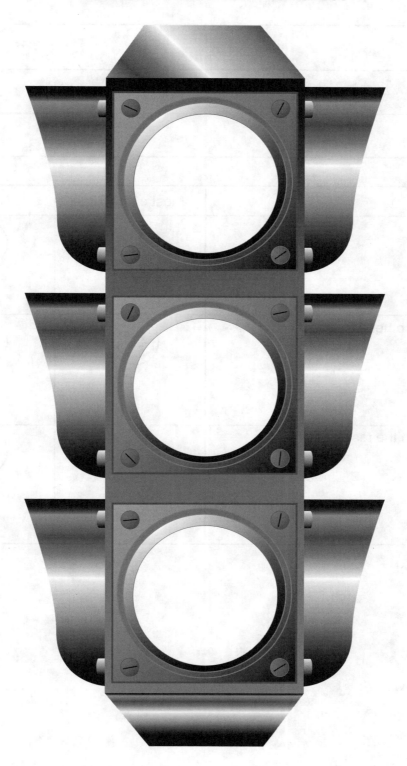

Blackline Master 12

Group Work Self-Reflection for Younger Students

Name:		
Date:		
Group Job:		

	Most of the Time	Not Yet
I did my job.	🙂	🙁
I listened to others.	🙂	🙁
I helped with the task.	🙂	🙁

I am proud of:

Next time, I will:

Blackline Master 13
Group Work Self-Reflection for Older Students

Name:
Date:
Group Job:

	Yes	Still Working At It	I know this because...
I performed my role.			
I listened to others.			
I cooperated with others.			
I helped complete the task.			
*Are there any others you want to add?			

Something I am proud about in my work on this group task is:

Something I would like to work on during the next group task is:

Blackline Master 14

Balancing Ways of Differentiating

Jot down a note about lessons, or simply shade or place a check mark in the squares to indicate how lessons were differentiated, and in what way.

Readiness	Interest	Learning Profile

Blackline Master 15
Anticipation Guide

Topic: _____

Before Learning   After Learning

Agree	Disagree		Agree	Disagree
		Idea: **Support It:**		
		Idea: **Support It:**		
		Idea: **Support It:**		
		Idea: **Support It:**		

Blackline Master 16

Door Pass

Door Pass

Name _____

Door Pass

Name _____

Blackline Master 17
H-Diagram

Topic:
_____

Topic:
_____

Similarities:

Blackline Master 18

W, W, W, W, and H Web

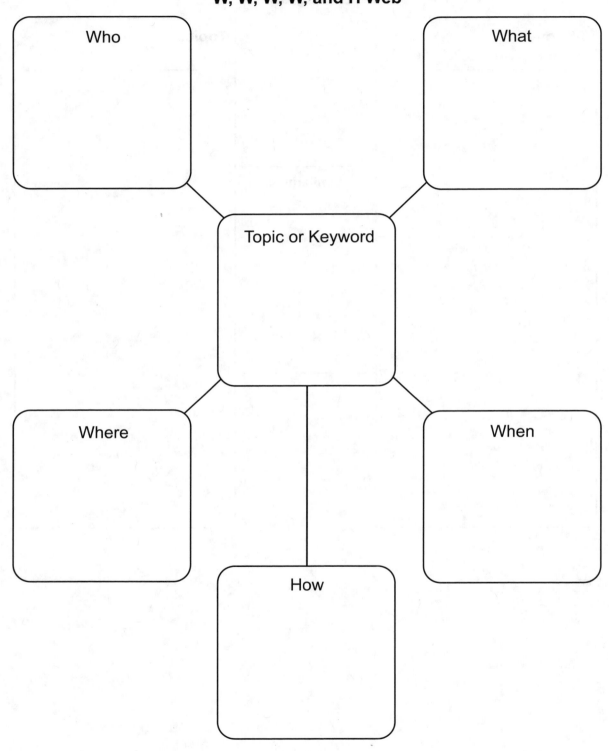

Who

What

Topic or Keyword

Where

When

How

Blackline Master 19

Tiered Lesson Plan Template

The Big Picture of the Lesson: Concept, Skills, Essential Questions, Enduring Understandings or Standard	Preassessment	Materials
	Grabber & Hook	
	Instruction	
Basic Tier	**Grade-Level Tier (START HERE)**	**Advanced Tier**
The students will _____ *(Verb)* _____ *(Specific Content)* Assessment:	The students will _____ *(Verb)* _____ *(Specific Content)* Assessment:	The students will _____ *(Verb)* _____ *(Specific Content)* Assessment:
Closure:		

Bloom's Taxonomy Verbs From Top Down (1 of 2)

Level Symbol	Synonyms	Products	Verbs	Question Stems
Synthesis **Create It!**	Inferring, creating, combining, developing, rearranging, reorganizing, generalizing, drawing conclusions	Inventions, campaigns, goals, game, poem, song or rap, research project, experiment, advertisement, tall tales, allegories	Compose, invent, create, design, build, construct, combine, plan, revise, propose, organize, originate, hypothesize, what if?, generalize, rewrite	■ What would happen if…? ■ What would happen next? How can you design, invent, compose, or arrange ____? ■ Can you propose alternative solutions and arrangement? ■ What changes would you make to solve…? ■ How would you improve it? ■ What do you think would happen if…? ■ How would you modify the plot or plan? ■ What could be done to minimize/maximize…? ■ Can you formulate a theory for…?
Evaluation **Judge It!**	Supporting, defending, criticizing, rating, prioritizing, discriminating, assessing, choosing, feeling	Listing the best and worst, book review, editorial, survey, debate, speech, list of trends, debate, awards, opinions, obituaries, critiques	Decide, judge, recommend, grade, rate, predict, critique, value, rank, assess, justify, convince, consider, persuade, recommend, summarize, choose, discriminate, support	■ Do agree or disagree and why? ■ How do you feel about ____ and why? ■ How would you justify, rate, evaluate, defend the importance of…? ■ Which is better and which is worse? ■ How would you prioritize or rank…? ■ Do you think ____ is a good example of ____, why or why not? ■ Based on what you know, how would you explain ____? ■ Which solution is the best and why?
Analysis **Sort It!**	Sorting, organizing, labeling, categorizing, contrasting, comparing, analyzing, distinguishing, sequencing	Collection, survey, questionnaire, graph, PowerPoint presentation, checklist, mindmaps, collections, debate, solving a mystery, metaphors, similes, and analogies	Inspect, analyze, compare, classify, dissect, examine, research, infer, conclude, interpret, contrast, categorize, survey	■ How would you organize ____ to show ____? ■ What are the features, parts, section, properties, characteristics of…? ■ How is ____ related to ____? ■ Why did ____ happen? How? ■ What ideas justify…? ■ What steps are important in the process of…? ■ How does ____ compare or contrast to ____? ■ How would you sort and label these groups of words?

Bloom's Taxonomy Verbs From Top Down (2 of 2)

Level Symbol	Synonyms	Products	Verbs	Question Stems
Application Do It!	Applying, relating, connecting, solving, transferring	Journal entries, news story, pamphlet, timeline, simulation, teach a lesson, demonstration, puppet shows, autobiographies, anecdotes	Apply, dramatize, illustrate, interview, build, choose, produce, prepare, demonstrate, solve, use, discover, calculate, experiment	■ How would you use…? ■ What examples can you find to…? ■ What approach or technique would you use to…? ■ How would you demonstrate…? ■ What else could ____ have done? ■ What do you think ____ would have done if ____? ■ How would you apply what you have just learned? ■ What result if…?
Comprehension Got it!	Understanding, interpreting, summarizing, explaining, describing, rewording, paraphrasing	Illustrations, TV bulletin, show and tell, oral report, visual with captions, chart, diorama, headlines or titles, want ads, biographies, letters, brochures	Describe, discuss, explain, retell, translate, reword, rewrite, extend, predict, match, paraphrase, interpret, illustrate, give examples	■ How would you explain or describe…? ■ How would you rephrase…? ■ Can you elaborate or give details to …? ■ Can you summarize or retell…? ■ What is the main idea…? ■ Which statements support…? ■ Can you explain what is meant by…?
Knowledge Know it!	Recalling, remembering, identifying, defining	Test, quiz, lists, pictures, 5W's, map, dictionary, trivia, memos, recipes	Tell, define, list, name, memorize, label, repeat, describe, identify, outline, select, identify, match	■ What do you know about…? ■ Can you define, list, recall or identify…? ■ How did ____ happen? ■ Who, what, where, when, questions.

Blackline Master 21

Product Choices

The followings is a list of some of the ways students could process what they are learning.

experiment	web boards	last will and testament
cubing	Wikis	Email
bumper sticker	debate	children's book
recipe	timeline	venn diagram
classified ad	love letter	WebQuests™
blog	storytelling	joke
comic book	talk show	PowerPoint™
audiotape	database	costumes
dance	fairy tale	brochure
slogan	interview	editorial
diary/journal	petition	riddles
videotape/digital video	puppet show	code creation/cracking
drama	speech	web page
comic strip	review	skit
flyer	graph	Project cube
invention	mind map	sketch book
Kidspiration/Inspiration™	job description	chart
podcast	wanted poster	poem
mock trial	animation	biography
obituary	photos/digital photos	readers theatre
online survey	monologue	magazine advertisement
pantomime	model	role play
learning contract	collections	collage
RAFT	survey	personal ad
picture dictionary	press conference	mural
poster	group discussion	sculpture
public service announcement	recycled art	newspaper
rap	map	nursery rhyme
scavenger hunt	demonstration	real-world problem
scrapbook	letter	song
sign	announcement	newscast
spreadsheet	game board	fact file
telecollaborative project	thank you note	advice column
travelogue	complaint	reflections
invitation	wedding vows	topic cube

Blackline Master 22

Dear Teacher Notes

Date _____

Dear Teacher,

_____

_____

_____

_____

Your Student,

Date _____

Dear Teacher,

_____

_____

_____

_____

Your Student,

Blackline Master 23
Personal Reflection

Personal Reflection

Topic or Skill: _____

1. How would you rate your background knowledge on this topic or skill before the lesson?

   ☐ I knew a lot

   ☐ I knew a little

   ☐ I didn't know much

2. Check all the ways that you processed this topic or skill during the lesson.

   ☐ Discussed it with one person

   ☐ Discussed it with several people

   ☐ Wrote about it

   ☐ Webbed it

   ☐ Played a game about it

   ☐ Created a product about it

3. Check all of the ways that you deepened your understanding of this topic or skill:

   ☐ Read a book

   ☐ Read a journal or magazine article

   ☐ Searched and read on the Internet

   ☐ Reviewed notes from teacher

   ☐ Viewed a video or DVD

   ☐ Read the newspaper

   ☐ Discussed with others (peers, family, teacher, expert)

   ☐ Other: _____

4. How do you know that your work/processing is accurate?

   ☐ Peer editing

   ☐ Compared it with something

   ☐ Teacher checked work

   ☐ Did additional research

   ☐ Used the following resource: _____

5. What was the most valuable/interesting/surprising aspect of what you learned?

_____

_____

_____

6. Now that I have processed what I've learned, I think I need to do one of the following:

□ Ask more questions about the concept in order to improve my understanding.

□ Continue at the pace I'm going.

□ Extend my learning because I understand it and want to learn more.

7. Next time I process, I would like to: _____

_____

_____

_____

(Jensen & Nickelsen, 2008)

References

Adams, C. J., & Pierce, R. L. (2003). Teaching by Tiering. *Science and Children, 41*(3), 30–34.

Allen, L. G., & Nickelsen, L. (2008). *Making Words Their Own: Building Foundations for Powerful Vocabularies.* Peterborough, NH: Crystal Springs Books.

Council of Administrators of Special Education Inc. (2008). *Case Response to Intervention.* Retrieved June 1, 2009 from http://www.casecec.org/rti.htm.

Costa, A., & Kallick, B. (2000). *Habits of Mind.* Alexandria, VA: Association for Supervision and Curirculum Development.

Diamond, M., & Hopson, J. (1998). *Magic Trees of the Mind.* New York: Dutton.

Fisher, D., & Frey, N. (2007). *Checking for Understanding: Formative Assessment Techniques for Your Classroom.* Alexandria, VA: Association for Supervision and Curirculum Development.

Gareis, C. R., & Grant, L. W. (2008). *Teacher-Made Assessments: How to Connect Curriculum, Instruction, and Student Learning.* Larchmont, NY: Eye On Education.

Heacox, D. (2002). *Differentiating Instruction in the Regular Classsroom: How to Reach and Teach All Learners, Grades 3–12.* Minneapolis, MN: Free Spirit Press.

Jacobs, B., Schall, M., & Sceibel, A. B. (1993). A quantitative dendritic analysis of wenicke's area in humans: Gender, hemispheric and environmental factors. *Journal of Comparative Neurology, 327*, 83–111.

Jensen, E. (2005). *Teaching With the Brain in Mind.* Alexandria, VA: Association for Supervision and Curirculum Development.

Jensen, E. (2008, December 6). Personal interview. (L. Nickelsen, interviewer.)

Jensen, E., & Nickelsen, L. (2008). *Deeper Learning: 7 Powerful Strategies for In-Depth and Longer Lasting Learning.* Thousand Oaks, CA: Corwin Press.

Kettler, T., & Curliss, M. (2003). Applying a tiered objectives model. *Gifted Child Today, 26*(1), 52–55.

Kingore, B. (2005). *Differentiating Instruction: Rethinking Traditional Practices.* Alexandria, VA: Association for Supervision and Curirculum Development.

Marzano, R. (2000). *Transforming Classroom Grading.* Alexandria, VA: Association for Supervision and Curriculum Development.

Marzano, R. J., Pickering, D., & Pollock, J. E. (2001). *Classroom Instruction that Works: Research-Based Strategies for Increasing Student Achievement.* Alexandria, VA: Association for Supervision and Curriculum Development.

McMackin, M. C., & Witherell, N. L. (n.d.). *Different Routes to the Same Destination: Drawing Conclusions with Tiered Graphic Organizers.* (International Reading Association, Ed.) 242–252.

McMackin, M. C., & Witherell, N. L. (2003). Using differentiated activities to enhance comprehension of all learners. *New England Reading Association Journal, 39*(2), 11–15.

Padgett, D. A., MacCallum, R. C., & Sheridan, J. F. (1998). Stress exacerbates age related decrements in the immune response to an experimental influenza viral infection. *Journals of Gerontology Series A: Biological Science and Medical Science, 54*(4), B347–B353.

Popham, W. J. (2008). *Transformative Assessment*. Alexandria, VA: Association for Supervision and Curirculum Development.

Rakow, S. (2007). All means all: Classrooms that work for advanced learners. *National Middle School Association Magazine, 11*(1), 10–12.

Restak, R. (2003). *The New Brain: How the Modern Age is Rewiring Your Mind*. Rodale Press.

Richards, M. E., & Omdal, S. N. (2007). Effects of tiered instruction on academic performance in a secondary science course. *Journal of Advanced Academics, 18*, 424–452.

Scott, B., & Turville, J. (1999). *Multi-Level Spelling Instruction*. Napanee, ON: On the Mark Press.

Sprick, R. S., Garrison, M., & Howard, L. (1998). *CHAMPs: A Proactive and Positive Approach to Classroom Management*. Longmont, CA: Sopris West.

Stetson, R., Stetson, E., & Anderson, K. A. Differentiated instruction, from teachers' experiences. *School Administrator, 64*(8), 28.

Stiggins, R. J. (2000). *Student-Centered Classroom Assessment* (3rd ed.). Upper Saddle River, NJ: Prentice Hall.

Suarez, D. When students choose the challenge. *Educational Leadership, 65*(3), 60–65.

Tomlinson, C. A. (1999). The Differentiated *Classroom: Responding to the Needs of All Learners*. Alexandria, VA: Association for Supervision and Curirculum Development.

Tomlinson, C. A. (2001). *How to Differentiate in Mixed-Ability Classrooms*. Alexandria, VA: Association for Supervision and Curriculum Development.

Tomlinson, C. A. (2009). *The Differentiated Classroom: Responding to the Needs of All Learners*. Alexandria, VA: Association for Supervision and Curirculum Development.

Tomlinson, C. A., & Strickland, C. A. (2005). *Differentiation in Practice: A Resource Guide for Differentiating Curriculum Grades 9–12*. Alexandria, VA: Association for Supervision and Curirculum Development.

Uchino, B., Cacioppo, J., & Kiecolt-Glaser, J. (1996). The relationship between social support and physiological process: A review with emphasis on underlying mechanisms and implications for health. *Psychological Bulletin, 119*, 488–531.

Vygotsky, L. S., Rieber, R. W., & Carton, A. S. (1988). *The Collected Works of L.S. Vygotsky: Volume 1: Problems of General Psychology, Including the Volume Thinking and Speech (Cognition and Language: A Series in Psycholinguistics)*. New York: Plenum Press.

Wiggins, G., & McTighe, J. (2005). *Understanding by Design* (2nd ed.). Upper Saddle River, NJ: Prentice Hall.

Witherell, N., & McMackin, M. (2002). *Graphic Organizers for Differentiated Instruction in Reading*. New York, NY: Scholastic.

Wormeli, R. (2003). *Day One & Beyond*. Portland, ME: Stenhouse.

Wormeli, R. (2006). *Fair Isn't Always Equal: Assessing & Grading in the Differentiated Classroom*. Portland, ME: Stenhouse Publishers.

Wormeli, R. (2007). *Differentiation: From Planning to Practice Grades 6–12*. Portland, ME: Stenhouse Publishers.